The Draft

Jemima Elizabeth Layzell

This precious diary represents Jemima's view of the world she lived in for far too short a time. For those who knew her it will shine new light on their memories and for those who did not know her it will serve as an intimate insight to the life of a child of today. To have been mentioned in her diary as a writer who she enjoyed reading is a delight to me, and to be asked to write this foreword is a huge honour. We all have our stories to tell. Some of us live long enough to tell many of them. This is Jemima's first and last and because of that so important to all of us who read it now. This is her life.

Michael Morpurgo

I think it's the most beautiful, touching, heart-breaking book. It must be so devastating to lose such a wonderful talented child – but clearly this precious book is one way that she will live on in everyone's hearts.

Jacqueline Wilson

Dedicated to all those who have made the world a better place, and to those who never had a chance to.

Thanks You

ACKNOWLEDGMENTS

Jemima loved school and regarded learning as an exciting part of life's challenges and pleasures. For this we thank all the staff at Ashill Community Primary School and Taunton School, especially Andy Manners, Jemima's English teacher, who gave her courage to write freely and on her own terms.

To the medical teams in Musgrove, Frenchay and the Bristol Children's Hospital for their dedication and skill in treating Jemima with such faith and compassion even when we knew all hope had gone, we are enormously grateful.

Love and gratitude to our friends and family, particularly Dom Denny who gave us strength to see this project completed.

Thanks are also due to Sophie Beveridge, Grania Coleman, Caro Ness, Anita Clare Field, Vickie Hobbs, Jacqueline Wilson and Michael Morpurgo.

Jemima referred to her last diary as 'The Draft', hence the title of this book.

FOREWORD

Jemima was lovely — clever, funny, compassionate and creative. She was a great artist but planned to be an author and left many poems, songs, stories and as well as serious thoughts about her life and the world's problems and delights. All her work here has been reproduced with only minimal corrections to punctuation and spelling as we felt that it's important to hear Jemima's voice first hand. The photographs have been added by us.

Most of the time Jemima was quite serious, but she also enjoyed silly games like consequences, treasure hunts and tree climbing. She usually carted around a large bag with school essentials, her private diary and several books. On the day she died the books were Milton's *Paradise Lost* and *The Right to Write* by Julia Cameron.

She was deep, at times unfathomable and somewhat troubled, partly by 'voices' and inner demons and partly because she was a rapidly-blossoming teenager, trying to make sense of and find her place in the world.

Before her death she had mentioned her wish to be an organ donor when she died. We had no idea that shortly after this we would be asked to honour this wish. Eight people have benefited from vital parts of her beautiful young healthy body, of which five are children.

This book is for you, Jemima, so your dream of becoming a published author has come true, and it's for all those who will never meet you in person, so they can get to know the person we loved and mourn our loss with us.

Live   Love   Laugh

Harvey, Sophy and Amelia Layzell
May 2013

This Diary belongs to Jemima Elizabeth Layzell

If I were a Fairy I'd be called Lizzy Stardust

Interesting facts about me:

I am 10 years old

My birthday is 21st May 1998

I have dark brown hair

I have brown eyes

I am 4 foot 5 inches tall

My favourite food is jacket potato cheese and beans

My favourite colour is red

My favourite animals are elephants and dolphins

My favourite hobby is reading

My most secret wish is for somebody to really, really like me for who I am.

I am really good at reading, writing, art, singing, and being a brill friend.

The friend I've known for longest is Gracie.

She is 10 years old, she is 4 foot 7 inches. Her birthday is on 24th September 1998, she has blue eyes and blonde hair.

The day we first met was before we went to playgroup. We were made for each other back then. We walked right up to each other.

We're best friends because we always have been and we are always there.

Gracie is really good at singing and being fun.

Jemima's first day at Ashill C P School, with Amelia aged 2.

TUESDAY 4th SEPTEMBER 2007

Amelia my Outstanding Little Sister

- She has great friends
- When I'm down she is one of the only ones I can talk to
- She is confident
- She plays games with me
- She is always looking after me
- She shares
- She always keeps secrets
- She almost always understands
- We get on

I was really sad for ages. No one could cheer me up. When my sister Amelia just touched me I felt as if I hadn't been sad in the first place. She cuddled and kissed me and I felt happier than I had ever felt before! Because I feel safe with her, because of her qualities,

I love my little sister Amelia Catherine Rose Layzell

SEPTEMBER 2007

Why doesn't Mum ever choose me? [1] I deserved that part and she knows it, she just doesn't want to choose me because I'm her daughter. She says I have a wonderful voice so why isn't she giving me a chance to let people know that. She's the only one who's realized, so why not give me a part that can show people like Mr Scotney and Grace (Gracie sorry) who I really am. Why is she trying to hide my abilities? Or perhaps she's lying and I have an awful voice? Whichever it is, I'm going to find out. No-one hails MY parade!

---

[1] Sophy Layzell ran a drama club called MAdD, now called MaKe.

The Book for Girly Girls

Intro: Hello, welcome. Here you will find out how to be popular, pretty, polite, gentle and helpful etc.

Top Tip: Remember your parents love you and tell you off for your own good.

NEVER

Get a boyfriend until 16 or over (18 at best). They will annoy in class and get you into trouble and it's not suitable!

ALWAYS

Stay calm and relaxed and patient plus don't lose your temper.

Top Tip: Try not to leave things to the last minute.

15th May 2005, Jemima with Gracie at her 7th birthday party.

JUNE 2008

I'm so Sorry Mr Scotney

Dear Mr Scotney

Please do not read this letter out loud. I am afraid to say I have not done my homework this weekend, when I was so very looking forward to it. You may think I have been a disgrace, and if you do, you are totally correct. I have been most silly and stupid.

Mum said we couldn't go back because Melie [2] was already late for violin. When we got home we found Mr Timms [3] had forgotten. We tried to ring him, but we could not get hold of him. I asked Mum if we could go back now, but she said it would be a waste of petrol, so we didn't go back.

Do you know what? I would love to do it at playtime, but wouldn't you rather [let] me finish my story? I really want to make up for what I've done. Maybe take it on holiday for me to finish? Don't get worked up about a mistake. Everyone forgets sometimes.

So let's just put the past behind us and forget about it. Promise you won't be mad? We all learn from mistakes. You can be mad if you want but I don't mind, 'cause I'm writing this letter to show that I care!

BEAT THAT! Mr Scotney, my hopes are upon you,

Jemima

Ps. Please excuse my wonky lines.

Pps. Same with the handwriting

Ppps. Are there any spelling mistakes?

---

[2] Amelia.

[3] The violin teacher.

JULY 2008

We'll never forget what we have learnt here [Ashill School]. How to listen, how to be kind, how to be helpful and how to use our mind to make friends, what is right and what is wrong.

We'll miss the teachers who helped us on the way, they always give us a lot of attention and help. We'll never forget what our friends have done.

1st Lani, remember the invention!

2nd Grace my BFF always

3rd Lauren she's so very kind to us

4th Katie to whom we'll forever be Pengi face and Pengi-face junior

5th Beth who plays and jokes with us and

6th Alice she always keeps secrets and last but not least

7th Madeline for being there for my sister.

Our friends mean more than anything to us, we will always be together looking out for each other. In our hearts we'll always see you, let our friendships never die. We want to tell you not to be afraid to show who you really are. Be who you want to be, no one's stopping you.

Ashill CP Sports Day

Jemima (r) aged 10 and Amelia 8 on their first day at Taunton School, 2008

WEDNESDAY 17th DECEMBER 2008

[A holiday to Barbados]

6.30 am Get up to find my sister moaning, my Dad half-dressed and my Mum fussing. Dear oh dear!

6.40 am I'm dressed washed and wheeling the suitcases down the [hotel] corridor.

6.45 am The *** suitcase gets stuck for the 15 millionth time.

7.05 am We have hopped on a bus and are now stuck in the South Terminal in a queue.

7.15 am Still stuck in a queue

7.40 am We finally get past . . . Oh no, more security.

8.20 am We, well Mum decides to go shopping for perfume.

8.27 am Mum and Dad argue

8.30 am We shop again

9.10 am We eat. I have apple juice and this lush cheesey thing with tomato, ham and pastry. Yum

9.35 am I go to the loo. Yuck! There's wee all over the seat!

9.40 am We try to find our gate

10.01 am We find our gate

10.30 am We get through our gate

7.07 am [reset watches to Barbados time] We take off

7.10 am We open our presents from Grandma

9.55 am We watch Mamma Mia

3.30pm We land

6.20 pm We arrive at our hotel.

Dear Diary

Dad's in a much better mood now he can open his suitcase. I am very happy with our room. I'm sitting on the balcony now listening to the waves crashing onto the beach. It's very dark now but very hot.

Apparently it's going to rain, but Dad says tropical rain is very warm so I hope we're swimming if and when it does. I feel very relaxed though I don't know what the time is. At home it's probably like midnight and I actually feel quite tired.

Hi Diary again, we had supper and the food was quite surprising. After that we had a stroll along the beach and mum got bitten by an ant! Ha, ha! Anyway I think it's time to go to bed. Good night Diary.

THURSDAY 18th DECEMBER 2008

Dear Diary

We're about to walk along the beach hopefully without the ants! After that we're going to have breakfast, I wonder what's on the menu.

Oh, I forgot to tell you last night that we found out that these little silvery coloured frogs about **O** big made the mysterious tweeting noise.

Actually I found out, not we! But anyway, it's raining! It's not as hot as it was last night but still humid. On the balcony right now you can see little birdies hobbling on the beach. Bye for now Diary!

Diary, we've just seen a mother and baby otter! Well we thought they were otters at first but then we saw their bushy tails and now we don't know what they are. We're watching tele now, I had bacon, pancakes and two croissants and hot milk and sugar for breakfast. I've got to go now. See ya!

Dear Diary, it rained again and flooded everywhere! It was awesome. Then we boringly went to stupid gym. If this **O** is my foot **Ō** that's on average the water level, it didn't get inside too much, but it still did. I had chips, lemonade, pasta pizza and even more chips for lunch.

I have genius-ly predicted that this diary will take up 33 pages! Ha beat that!

Oopz Melie is going to kill me (I'm using her paper you see)

Tragedy! Dad trod on a snaily waily.

Moving on, for supper I had spaghetti in tomato and basil sauce.

In one of the pools there are two water slides and a Jacuzzi type thing and it was so cool. I gotta get washed now and Melie's being really wimpy about the snails! Hey, I can move my big toe separately to my other toes. Ha!

FRIDAY 19th DECEMBER 2008

Dear Diary

I've been for a walk along the beach this morning and I built a sandcastle and a pool of love! I splashed in the sea and dad did some skimming. Me and Dad had so much fun. I'm glad Melie and Mum didn't come they would have been spoil sports.

Breakfast was lush. After the yummy meal we went into town. We went into the museum and it had a talking pirate and a fake hurricane. Then we went into a cafe and had yum smoothies. We came back to our hotel and swam. Me and my sister played a game where we were having swimming lessons. We then had lunch followed by more swimming and a dip in the sea. But right now mum's telling me off for being slow. See ya!

I can't believe Mum's so obsessed with whether I pooed today. I mean like, come on, I am seriously full of food today and Dad is so fussy about drinking (alcoholic and non).

I forgot to tell you about the art gallery when we went into town. Some of the pictures were soooo realistic and others just looked amazing. Though some were just plain boring. Well, I gotta go to bed now, night night!

SATURDAY 20th DECEMBER 2008

Dear Diary

I am so excited about the submarine today. Just an hour to go, and 5 days till Christmas. I still can't believe I'm here. I built a sandman, (instead of a snowman).

Melie's getting in a strop about me using her paper. I really want to go scuba diving. Melie can't even snorkel! At the moment the sea looks so blue. Sorry, I'm being kind of random here. It took me ages to get up this morning. It's boiling here!

Dear Diary

I feel utterly sick!

I have found out that:

a)   People here don't usually bother about wearing seat belts.

b)   Not many people go in cars

c)   With turtles, one breath can last up to 47 hours!

d)   One type of fish can mate up to 10 times a day!

e)   Another fish can change gender!

f)   'We all live in a yellow submarine…' Submarines can be big

g)   Palm trees can be massive

h)   My sister can be an idiotic pig

i)   All drinks have tonnes of ice.

j)   I have yellow sticky puss on my leg [4]

k)   Side leg raisers hurt!

Dear Diary,

Mum said that last night I was fidgeting madly and when I woke up the covers had fallen off the bed. The submarine was awesome. Pizza and chips for lunch. I did some snorkelling in the pool, pasta and lamb for supper, coconut water too (which I spat out all over mum!) Anyway time to go to sleep now bye!

SUNDAY 21st DECEMBER 2008

Dear Diary

20 past 6 at the mo. I'm on the balcony now. Everyone is so friendly. The sea looks nice and calm today. Dad said I could go snorkelling with my flippers on in the sea.

Dear Diary, I've been snorkelling in the sea and I saw millions of fish. Yesterday when we went to the submarine there was a man dressed up as Santa Claus and he was really funny. He kindly gave us a bag of sweets. I had two croissants for breakfast with pineapple and peach for pudding thing. Before I had gone in the sea we went in the pool. Right now I'm just waiting for lunch.

---

[4] Jemima's spelling of pus.

Lunch was yum. I had chips, pizza carrots and a fruit salad. Then we went snorkelling in the sea and pool. We're at the gym now watching Dad do press ups at the speed of light. There's this really weird music going on at the mo. See you later.

Dear Diary, I've just had a bath. I found a penny, well a cent. It was made this year as well. It's very shiny. We're about to go to supper now, I'm v. hungry, see ya!

MONDAY 22nd DECEMBER 2008

I'm sorry I didn't speak to you last night. I was well tired. For supper I had chips, pizza and veggies. Melie didn't drink enough and refused to drink this special hydrating stuff. I've got to go to breakfast. Byeee!

Dear Diary, I've just been writing postcards to my grandparents. I'm doing some crosswords right now and Granny's birthday prezzie. I had bacon, pancakes and fruit for breakfast. I've been swimming in the pool but I'm out now. Hey, is that Mum calling me for lunch?

Dear Diary, we've moved camp and are now on the beach. I've been snorkelling in the sea and Dad got cut on both knees! There's a bride and groom here and they're having photos taken on the beach. I like it here in Barbados. Lunch was nice. I had chips, pizza, carrots and some form of vegetable and a fruit salad. Dad now says we have to have half a cup of water every half an hour! Mum and Meils have gone for a walk. I wonder when supper is, I'm hungry.

Mum keeps finding all these snail shells and pieces of glass. She's made a massive collection now no one can put anything else on the table. Oh look, here comes Mum and the weed back from their walk. What! Melie's found a toy tardis! The sun's setting right now. The sky is green! I gotta go now. I hope its supper.

Poop! Just off for a shower it will be at least 20 mins before supper. I didn't have time to tell you earlier, but we went on a banana boat, it was so cool. Yippy! Supper at long last.

TUESDAY 23rd DECEMBER 2008

Dear Diary

I'm so sorry I didn't speak to you last night, I was so tired. Dad says it's because of the pill I took. Pumpkin fritters are absolutely, extremely delicious! I had them last night along with a disgusting fish cake and a weird macaroni pie, and disgusting jugjug [5] thing. I gotta go Dad's getting mad.

Dear Diary, breakfast was nice. I had pineapple, pancakes, croissants; yoghurt and toast with corn beef.

I've just been swimming with turtles! It was cool. There were loads of them, when they came up to me, I felt like hugging them and playing with them forever. It was magical, even though Melie was a wimp. By the time she went into the water it was time to go back. Anyway diary, I think I'll go and read now, see ya!

Dear Diary, I'm on the beach. I've just been to the medical centre because after we went swimming with turtles I went in the sea with Dad and I got stung. Dad said I was very brave, but I don't see how I was. Anyway we're about to have lunch now, bye.

Dear Diary, I'm by the pool. Lunch was weird. I had a hot dog which was disgusting, chips and sweetcorn with macaroni. I've been in the pool and Dad's been throwing me 15 million mini mm into the air then laughing at me as I drop with a big splash into the very deep pool. Bye I'm going now.

---

[5] Jug-jug is a traditional Bajan Christmas dish.

10.20pm CHRISTMAS EVE

Dear Diary

It's 10.20pm and today's been great. In the morning a baby sitter came to look after us, while Mum and Dad went to the capital, Bridgetown, until the kids' club started.

In kids' club Melie made a friend and we played games, watched tele and a clown came in and played some games with us. Then we had lunch. Then Mum and Dad came back and we were visited by a man dressed up as Santa Claus. He gave us presents and I got a pink back pack and a pretty brown bracelet. Soon after that we had supper. I found out that the people here don't say 'Are you ok?' they say, 'you good?'! We had supper at this show. It had fire-eaters, limbo dancers, dancers, singers, steel drum players and stilt walkers. It was amazing. I'm really tired now. I betta go to sleep now. The best day of the year!

[CHRISTMAS DAY]

Dear Diary, I'm by the pool now. Me and Melie had a shock at breakfast. Dad had placed some presents for us under the Christmas tree in the restaurant. Mum and Dad gave me a makeup set (a big one) a pretty little dress and three really good (well they sound good) books. I am v. Happy. Dad has gone off to complain about air conditioning and Melie is for some unknown reason numbering the pages of her notebook in messy handwriting. I'm going to read one of my books now, bye!

News flash, Dad says we are moving rooms . . . I repeat . . . moving rooms!
Diary it feels like Christmas is all over now I've had presents. Oooo, apparently we are going on a treasure hunt, bye!

Diary, It's the end of the day now. The treasure was good. Melie came third. Though I did help her a tiny bit. Then we did the breaking of the piñatas. That was fun. I only got to have one hit though but I got a bag of sweets! After that we sat round the pool and had a little swim. Then we had lunch, then went off to the beach quickly before preparing for supper. Supper was nice.

BOXING DAY

Dear Diary,

I fell asleep writing last night, sorry. We're on a 4x4 trip tour thing now but we've stopped for a bit. It was a very bumpy ride.

We have been in a cave next to the Atlantic Ocean. The Atlantic is so rough you would hardly believe it. The cave was really cool! Apparently, there's a tree which gives apple looking things but you wouldn't want to eat the apple thing. When it rains, if you stand under the tree you get really bad blisters. I wonder when lunch is . . .

Dear Diary, We've stopped for lunch. We've seen green monkeys! They were soo cute. I'm going now bye.

Dear Diary, we've been around St John's church. The view is wonderful. See ya!

Dear Diary, I'm by the sea now. The 4x4 trip was brill. I loved it. There are these flowers that just smell absolutely gorgeous. Wonderful smell. The people here, on words like 'three' they say 'tree'! They don't say 'th' they say 'tu'! I've had a dip in the pool after I came back. Oh look we're packing up now, I wonder if it's supper?

Dear Diary, we finally went to supper, I had pasta with salmon then beef with gravy. Right then, I'm going to sleep now.

SATURDAY 27th DECEMBER 2008

Dear Diary, this morning I felt really tired and couldn't be bothered to get up. Dad had already gone to the gym and had a shower by the time we woke up.

He refused to bring us breakfast in bed. So for breakfast I had two croissants, rather boring. We spent most of our day by the pool, but sometimes went along the beach.

We went snorkelling and saw some fish. Before supper I bought a little Reggae Dude, he's sooo cool and sooo cute.

Melie is obsessed with jewellery, Mum's obsessed with pooing, Dad's obsessed with drinking and apparently, I'm obsessed with you, dear Diary. What has become of the world. Melie has bought yet another piece of jewellery. We're going to get two white t-shirts bye.

Dear Diary, don't they say bad luck comes in threes?

Oh look, Melie's lost blanky, this could be funny. . . Dad hid him, again . . . Melie's taking ages to find him . . . He was in her bag! I'm feeling tired now. Bye! See ya Diary.

SUNDAY 28th DECEMBER 2008

Dear Diary,

Melie feels sick, Dad is telling everyone to get up, Mum's trying to go back to sleep and I'm moaning over my tummy. OK. Dad's shouting I betta get up.

Dear Diary. I've finished breakfast and I'm waiting for Melie to eat her orange. We're going to the kidz club today and are going to do tie-dying and sand art and we're going to have our hair braided. I'm so excited. Now we're by the pool. I've never noticed how beautiful it is here. We had to move pools 'cause Mum got scared a coconut might fall on us. And now she's scared that Dad and Melie won't be able to find us. They were somewhere else when we moved pools you see. I'm just waiting for kidz club to start. See ya!

Dear Diary we're about to have supper. I have not had my hair braided, I'm having it tomorrow, but Melie had hers done. It's a long story, I don't have much time at the moment. Dad is busy taking millions of photos. Ouch! I just banged into the wall.

Tie-dying was good, this is my T-shirt. And in sand art I did a picture of a deer leaping through a forest. I'm proud of them both. Gotta go!

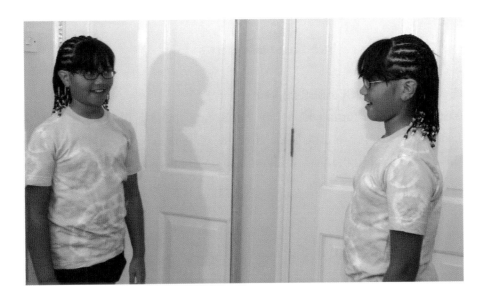

MONDAY 29th DECEMBER 2008

Dear Diary,

Today's been great. In the morning I had my hair braided in the Kidz Club when Mum and Dad went to the other hotel. I missed most of the activities and it took over two hours! The other ladies called the one doing my hair very slow. She kept saying 'Oh your hair is so lovely and tick (thick)' or 'you have so much hair'. While she was doing my hair it really hurt, but it feels really nice now. I have light blue and dark blue beads 'cause otherwise I might not be allowed it in school.

Everything has to be the school colours and the proper school hats, scarves, gloves, coats, badges, everything. Then mostly after that [it] was watching tele, playing on Nintendo, other boring bits and bobs until Mum picked us up after lunch. After that Dad tried to teach us to swim with flippers. It didn't work. Then we went back to the Kidz Club while Mum and Dad went to the Italian restaurant (adults only). We went crab hunting and saw millions of crabs. Then we watched this brill film about ice skaters. I'm feeling really tired I think I'll go to sleep.

Sorry I forgot. We had breadfruit for supper!

TUESDAY 30th DECEMBER 2008

Today we walked further along the beach and found a little bay and Melie made friends with two little black girls the same ages as us called Alisha and Alilia. We played in the sea with them and buried each other. In the afternoon we wanted to go on a chariot thing and we waited and waited and even more waiting until finally we could go on one. Dad and Mum hated it but I loved it!

WEDNESDAY 31st DECEMBER 2008

Dear Diary.

It's our last day today. We leave the hotel at 3:00 and fly back at 6:00. We're going to the Kidz Club today while Mum and Dad pack. Bye.

Dear Diary the Kidz Club were playing football so I built sandcastles with mini club and chatted to a five year old called Katelin. I'm going now.

After the Kidz Club we went down to the pool and me and Meils played Sunny and Penelope. Then we went along the beach and looked for glass and played in the sea without Dad. It has been really fun, our holiday, Diary, but I can't believe it's all over. Melie's just made up a song called 'Hot to freezing cold'.

Ah well, goodbye Barbados.

3:00 pm we leave the hotel

6:10 pm we get on the plane

11:20 pm we take off (late)

11:35 pm we watch tele 'Space Chimps'

1:02 am we go to sleep

5: 44 am we wake up

7:14 am we land

12:10 we drive home to our house.

JANUARY 2009

Night dream. We went on a school trip. Miss Andrews told us to shout '*****' when someone was chasing us. We built ships and sailed them to Barbados.

SATURDAY 31st JANUARY 2009

Dear Diary

I've been at Taunton School over a term now. I don't like it much there. I always look forward to Saturdays because I see some of my real friends at drama. I'm not deeply unhappy but I'd give almost anything to go back to Ashill, my old school. I was the most popular girl in the school at Ashill and at Taunton I just feel left out. You won't tell anyone will you. Anyway I gotta go now.

Boys are soo stupid. I once had a peep in the boy's toilets. I wish I'd worn a gas mask.

Diary, Katie's trying to do the hairstyle that Alice has got. It feels really nice. Now she's experimenting and it's going really well. She says she loves playing with hair. She's really good and I think she should be a hairdresser when she's older. She has really snazzy hairclips as well.

OMG [6]. . . sorry, just felt like saying that.

Apparently, we're all sleeping at Grandma's tonight. We're back home from drama now and I just need a toilet break a sec. . . .

I'm really hungry, aren't you? Mum and Dad are going to a party, that's why we're staying at Grandma's. I gotta go and pack my bag now.

SUNDAY 1st FEBRUARY 2009

Dear Diary

At Grandma's I had a great time. I wanted to stay up reading 'Private Peaceful' but I forgot my torch. My sister's usually extremely annoying but she was quite kind at Grandma's. I would have spoken to you earlier but we had to unpack, then have supper, then do homework so I haven't had a chance. We had a roast as usual. I love roasts, they are delicious. I love drawing and reading, especially when I do it up a tree. I don't know quite what I want to be when I grow up. Maybe I'll be an artist or a writer. I once considered singing, but now I can see, it's out of the question. I'm good, but not so good. Besides I'm far better at art.

MONDAY 2nd FEBRUARY 2009

Dear Diary

Today was like a blizzard. You should have seen it Diary. It was cool, cooler than cool. Amazing cool. All my sister ever does is: moan, fuss, pull faces, say no, and kick. She's so violent she is.

Moving on. . .

I'm falling behind a lot at school. All I want to do is sleep so I think I'll stop now. Goodnight.

---

[6] 'Oh My God'.

TUESDAY 3rd FEBRUARY 2009

Diary!

OMG! And I mean it this time. I've heard some of the best news ever. NO, no to school and Hello to sledging! Whoohoo! Catch you later.

On Windmill Hill with Lani.

Wow, wow and wow again. THAT was awesome. Best time in my life! (Well, almost. The best was the reunion of me and all my buddies at Ashill) I tried having a snowball fight with my sister but she just got all stroppy and told on me. She's always telling on me and getting me into trouble. Sometimes though I lie in a very clever way so that they believe me and then Melie (my sister) gets the blame.

Ouch! I've hurt my foot, but I don't know how. Mum suggested it might have been when I was taking my wellies off. I'm in bed now. Oh dear, I still haven't given Granny and Tony their Christmas present (that's because I was on holiday in Barbados over Christmas) I'm invited to a party as well, two in fact. One after the other. I'm getting tired. See ya soon!

WEDNESDAY 4th FEBRUARY 2009

Dear Diary

Melie's been giving me Chinese burns and they still hurt. She denies it though. She keeps calling me a big fat liar. But I'm quite small, quite thin and not a liar. I was off games today as I hurt my foot sledging yesterday. We missed a cake sale yesterday, but we made cookies at home which were lush. See you in the morning.

SATURDAY 7th FEBRUARY 2009

Dear Diary

I didn't go to school yesterday either. It was the deepest snow I've ever had in my life. Honest! I went up to Windmill Hill and met up with some of my friends. We went sledging and made a massive snowball. I've just been to a party. Emily's party, it was fab. I got to see all of my friends. It's very late but we left early. I think I'll go to sleep I've got another party tomorrow.

SUNDAY 8th FEBRUARY 2009

Dear Diary

It's still snowy outside but not as deep as yesterday. I'm hungry, I want some breakfast. Don't you? I won a packet of jelly tots yesterday, but I'm not too keen on jelly tots. I seem to have gone off sweets a bit. I'm reading a fab book by Michael Morpurgo, 'Private Peaceful' it's true what they say you know, any book with the words 'Michael Morpurgo' are guaranteed excellent quality. Or something like that anyway. I'm a big Michael Morpurgo fan.

Hera and Holli's party was good. We went to the Odeon in Taunton. We saw City of Ember, it was really good. Then we had a Chinese instead of a roast at this Mandarin place. Anyway I'm going to sleep now, bye.

TUESDAY 10th FEBRUARY 2009

Dear Diary

It was flooded everywhere. It took us 2 hours to get to school! And Mr Ward made up a rubbish joke about us swimming to school.

WEDNESDAY 11th FEBRUARY 2009

Dear Diary

Parents Evening today. If I had to list and label subjects, then it would look like this.

Art - Wow!

English - Excellent

Science - Excellent

Maths - very good

History - good

Geography - good

French - ok

RE - ok

ICT - Rubbish

DT [7] - Poor

oopz I forgot: PE and Games - ok

I do try my best though! Apparently, I'm doing well though.

March 2009. Pictures of Jemima and friends in 'Seussical'.

[7] ICT: Information Computer Technology, DT: Design Technology.

Lost

A sonnet by Jemima Layzell

I'm walking but I don't get anywhere

My destination seems so far away.

The darkness, do I enter, do I dare?

Like going backwards from the big bright ray.

I have to go alone, this is my fight,

I struggle onwards all the way through life.

I'm nearly out of dark, I see the light,

Like balancing barefoot on sharpened knife.

My path, so ugly that it's beautiful

Deceives me as I walk along its back.

There's no one left to say it's wonderful.

I have nothing, it's everything I lack.

How can a bird that's born for joy take wing,

Sit dying locked up in a cage and sing?

SUMMER 2009

Extract from Milly Jones Lucky You [8]

by Jemima Layzell

What have you done now Milly?!

Dad loves to go on a cycle ride: it's just his thing. Personally going on a cycle ride is not my thing. They're ok but to be honest I'd rather watch tele. Anyway Dad decided that this would be the right time to go to the canal and ride our bikes.

---

[8] This is based on real life!

I feel quite happy cycling along, until I come to a bridge, or a hill, or another person. Whenever we go on a cycle ride I always cycle in the middle, Dad at the front with my younger sister Daisy on the back of his bike, then me and Mum following on behind.

Dad and Daisy like to zoom off ahead leaving me and Mum to race with the snails. Right now Dad is telling us to keep up.

'Keep up!' see! So I move my gears up and pedal rather fast. Though apparently I have a habit of slowing down, since Mum [has a] habit of saying things like, 'keep going' or 'speed up'.

Here comes a hill. Do gears go up or down? Up, no down I think. Help! My gears seem to be stuck and I am losing control, plus I am in 3, 7 which is not good. So, I climb off and push my bike up the hill. Then I find it isn't so easy on the way down. It's a bit like taking Kiara on a walk and then she meets another dog. (Though she's been quite good recently)

Today's one of those days when you have a song stuck in your head and can't get it out of your head or stop yourself from singing it. So here I go!

'Are you ready, are ya ready for this are ya hanging on the edge of your seat?!' I find this rather a tongue twister so it came out more of a,

'Are ya ready, are ya reday for this are ya hangy on de shhhhhseat?!' kind of thing. So I tried it again and I said it correctly. Then I stopped I didn't know the rest.

Mum is now telling me to slow down because we are coming to a bridge. I don't like bridges because you have to go underneath them on a narrow path. I have to admit I'm rather nervous. But I stay calm because Mum says accidents happen when you're nervous. It must be easier going the other way because the way we're going the path goes up to a bridge and then down towards the canal before a sharp turn under the bridge on a narrow path. This path is a particularly narrow one.

I slow right down and I think I've made it! But then it's all cold. I'm falling. I see a shimmering. A beautiful shimmering. Above me, above the murkiness, a figure, running above the shimmering. I think I'm dreaming. Yes. That's it. It's exactly how it is in my dreams. I'm sinking. Slowly sinking.

I-I-I-I- can't breathe. I've just realised. That means I'm not dreaming. I can always breathe underwater in my dreams. I need to get out. I must have fallen in the canal. No! This is not me. Only a fool would fall in the canal. Besides my lucky charm would never let a thing like this happen to me. Or would it? I remember now I left my lucky charm at home.

I am utterly out of breath and standing here by a patch of stinging nettles, wearing my spare cardigan and Daisy's top, dripping like a total idiot.

Dad's off finding a branch to hook my bike out of the canal. The bike is upside down in the water. I feel soo utterly stupid. I mean just look at me. I am an idiot. Full stop.

[Extracts from a school notebook]

Jemima Layzell   Roberts 7P [9]

My friends, they are loyal and faithful and we have a very special bond, but my friends are free to be who they want to be. I have no power over that. I will let them do what they want to do. I will not stop them.

You are mixing stubbornness and anger with strength and the people will not like it.

---

[9] Her school house and form.

<u>Dreams</u>

My computer was attacked by Windows 7 Home premium. It turned off and turned it on. I tried to turn it off later on but it kept coming on again. Boxes appeared on the screen and a spider crawled across it singing ABBA. I screamed and woke up.

WEDNESDAY 17th JUNE 2009

Dear Diary

Help! I've got injections today! We're going to Phuket on the 5th July. The hotel looks amazing. I'm really looking forward to it. It's a 26 hour journey!

THURSDAY 18th JUNE 2009

Dear Diary

The injections didn't hurt but they hurt now.

SATURDAY 20th JUNE 2009

Dear Diary

It's Saturday today and really hot. Yesterday I went to Lauren's sleepover. It was just me, Lauren and Ffion. It was great! We watched two movies and had lots of sweets for a midnight feast. I'd just been to the summer fair and bought two things of candy floss. It was a smash!

I'm really tired and I've got Grace coming to stay in a minute. This morning was drama and it started 30 minutes late. It was fun though.

I really like saying, 'How unpredictable, yet predictable' and 'Don't you know anything' and 'Precisely'.

My Laguna Holiday Adventure

by Jemima Layzell

For my

wonderful sister

Amelia

Happy Birthday

L

O

V

E

Y

O

U

SATURDAY 4th JULY 2009

Dear Diary

Today we are packing our suitcases for holiday. We broke up from school the day before yesterday. We performed our play today. I've got to go got packing, see ya then.

Hi I'm back again. I'm making a list of clothes and stuff (well I'm about to)

2 x nightclothes

18 x knickers

6 x socks

3 x swimming costumes

1 x diary

1 x pen

1 x towelling dress

11 x dresses

11 x tops

5 x shorts

3 x skirts

1 x cardi

2 x trousers

4 x shoes

1 x hat

2 x toys

1 x Nintendo

1 x zen [10]

1 x book

1 x wash bag

1 x Nintendo charger

1 x tissues

2 x leggings

Hand luggage confirmed

Jewellery

1 x art book

I won't be speaking to you 'til on the plane see ya then.

MONDAY 6th JULY 2009

Dear Diary,

I'm so sorry I did not speak to you on the plane. We have to wait over an hour in this airport to wait for another plane to Phuket. I kept finding myself asleep and my head collapsed.

---

[10] A Zen is an mp3 portable music player.

I am opposite this man at the moment and where's he gone? Sorry I was day dreaming and then he, oh look, he's back now. Anyway he has this shopping bag which says 'discover the whole person,' I think I know what that means. Ah ha caught him in the act! Sorry, he left again. Back so soon. Please excuse me. Off again are you?

It's time for me to go too, I'll be back soon, and actually, I'll take you with me. Sorry I couldn't talk to you as unfortunately I was on the loo.

I'M so BORED . . . no offence.

Dear Diary, we're in our hotel room now and the hotel is amazing. I love it here. We're going off down to the pool in a sec. I'm in my bikini underneath my Barbados dress. Mum and Dad have argued already. Though I suppose no one's had any sleep. I barely caught a wink so I'm really tired but I can't wait to have fun. Melie's arranging her felt tips! I better help un-pack. See ya at the pool.

Soz! I left you behind. I forgot. Never mind. I still had a great time. I had a can of Fanta (orange) and suddenly a thousand wasps came out of nowhere and started drowning themselves in it. One got its head stuck in the straw! I'm meant to be having a nap so bye for now.

Dear Diary, I am sooooo hot. I couldn't get up after my nap somehow I did though. We have just been on a walk round the village and now at Andeman pool bistro which is a restaurant type thing. When Melie finally finishes her coconut we're going to one of the shacks. She's eating it tiny bit by tiny bit. She says it doesn't taste nice otherwise, of course it doesn't Melie!

We're at the TOM YUM GOONG restaurant. Hang on.

Dear Diary, we're over by the Reggae Bar. I've got some ice tea here and it's ok, but . . . nevermind. Anyway I swear I just saw something come out of the water, flip, then splash back down again. We're waiting for Melie, again!

TUESDAY 7th JULY 2009

Dear Diary

Dad stinks! He's now taking pictures of me talking to you.

Mum says we can go on a water taxi, then see the elephants at breakfast. Or something like that, or maybe it was the other way round.

Dear Diary

Do you like my elephants?

Thanks if you do. It was elephants first by the way. We went to the village on the water taxi. Dad's having a something made at the tailors, can't remember what it was. Breakfast was great. Oh, and I gotta speak to Grandma on the phone, I'll keep talking to you.

I just told Grandma about you. We're talking about the sea and food. I sneezed. The elephants had long hairs. Goodbye Grandma.

I've had walks along the beach but we can't go in the sea. Melie collected shells. She calls one type 'spiralies'. She's sweet. Did I just say that! No, I didn't, I wrote it! OK not funny right? OK so then we went in the pool and I played with Melie and went down the slide and played with these diving things. I wish I could eat diary.

Dear Diary. HI. Mum and Dad are talking to our rep. Phew, glad that's over. SUPPER! Here I come.

Boohoo Dad's forcing me to have a picture. Not more pictures. I'm hungry! Now people are telling me off for being hungry. No fair! Melie's knee stings (well, so she says) There's a half elephant half man statue with lots of stuff on it. Dad's taking a picture of it. How unpredictable yet predictable. Sorry, I like that line, I mean like, don't you know anything! Sorry, I like that line too. Oh look drinks! Wait a sec.

Jemima and her father rubbing noses.

Here again. We're discussing where to have supper. I wish someone would hurry up and make a decision. Oh look, Mum wants to go to a restaurant on the beach. Now we're talking about bears. Dolphins and elephants are my favourite animals.

Dear Diary, I'm sorry I left you in the room. We had supper. Sorry I left you. Night night.
Ps. Diary, my tongue got stuck to my ice lolly and my tongue feels really weird.
Pps. Dad takes pictures of absolutely everything!

WEDNESDAY 8th JULY 2009
Dear Diary
It's 'round about one o'clock. We have been in the pool all morning, we have to go for lunch now and I'm burning.

Dear Diary, It's almost supper now. Melie still absolutely refuses to go on the slide. Tomorrow we're going to the kids club. I'll see you after supper or I might take you. Depending.

Dear Diary, we are in the lobby now. A Thai woman is giving us drinks and snacks. Here they have these Pringle type things which aren't Pringles. I love it here. I love it, I love it, I love it. The peanuts are nice. Dad's smoking. It stinks. Mum's saying how Dad's got a girly giggle, but Papa [11] has a man laugh. The sky looks beautiful. I wish Melie wouldn't be so stupid and ignorant.

Dear Diary, Melie's had lots of orchids in her drinks and stuff and she's kept them and keeps dropping them. We're now sitting in the lobby again, by the bar listening to these Thai people singing English songs. They are really good.

---

[11] Jemima's paternal grandfather.

Oh, you know the half man, half elephant statue? It's a God, the elephant god, Ganesha. Or something like that.

Mum's all excited because it's a someone/something song.

Dad took a picture of a cockroach. Mum's now singing to 'When I'm 64'.

THURSDAY 9th JULY 2009

Dear Diary

Me and Dad got up early today and walked along the lagoon. Last night Dad snored like an elephant! It kept me awake for hours, then the next thing I know he's shaking my leg! Now I'm listening to Seussical on my zen. Mum's drying her hair. I'm hungry. Need Breakfast, we're ready and waiting for Mum, and, you guessed it, Melie.

Dear Diary, I have finished breakfast. We are still in here because we are waiting for Melie. How unpredictable! Mum's going to the loo. We're going to the kids' club.

Dear Diary, the elephant was next to dad and he didn't notice. The elephant drank the water from the water fountain. Mum wanted to draw a picture of the elephant in you but I wouldn't let her. I tried to send Dad down the lift again but it didn't work.

Dear Diary, kids' club was fine. Sorry I did not speak to you, I did not have time. There was this girl that reminded me of Molly Coleman. Her face looked the same, her voice was the same, and what she said was similar. We were the only ones staying for lunch, me and Amelia.

We are walking to the Tom Yam Goong restaurant and it's rather dark so I will have to stop talking to you.

Dear Diary, hi again. I'm at the Tom Yam Goong restaurant. We're all deciding what to have. Now where was I? Ah yes, so the activities were fun.

We went Kayaking. 'Scuse me a mo.

Hi again, sorry, I had to go and choose my fish.

We played with a girl and her sister. The older one was Franka and the younger ones name was Nynka. They're from Holland. They speak Dutch and English, they've lived in Australia for four years. Then we had lunch and afterwards we fed the elephant. Then we painted papier mâché, then watched tele and had tattoos done. The tattoos have almost gone now because of the mosquito repellent.

Anyway, then Mum and Dad picked us up and took us to the pool. It was the scuba pool and it's 3 metres deep.

One bit was shallow though, but it was like a cliff, it just dropped.

Oh look, food! Oh yes, I remember after kayaking we went swimming. After the scuba pool we went back to our room, while Dad went to the gym. Me and Melie played snakes and ladders. On the way down I got in a mood. It stayed until I drunk something at the bar and had some peanuts.

Dear Diary, supper was delicious. Especially the pudding. Well goodnight, tomorrow, Phi Phi Island.

FRIDAY 10th JULY 2009
Dear Diary
I'm on Bamboo Island. Mum Melie and Dad are on a walk. Ants keep crawling over the page. We have just had lunch and Melie was moaning about not going in the sea. Phi Phi Island was cool, but there were so many people.
There were even bottle tops floating in the sea. Dad said it wasn't as beautiful as he expected. We've been snorkelling. The boat goes really fast and the pineapple is really nice here. Pineapple tastes nice with coconut milk. The bananas here are really small, we fed them to the elephant yesterday.
I'm trying to squish all these ants. Sometimes I wish Melie wouldn't be such a worm. Everyone thinks she's so sweet.
Fake Melie 'Sweet Thing' Real Melie 'Devil'
Fake me 'Lunatic' Real Me 'Thinker'
Fake Dad 'Joker' Real Dad 'Shouter'
Fake Mum 'Smiler' Real Mum 'Reader'

Dear Diary, I'm in the room now. The boat journey on the way back was really rough and for once Melie wasn't sick.

Dear Diary, wow! I have used up 23 pages already. Right, now we are in the Chai Nam bar. I have had a Virgin Pinacolada and 4 ½ peanuts and 3 Pringle type things.

Sabardebar — hello

Khobkhumd

Khobkhun lai — thank you

Sorry, it's Lao. Long story. But if you really, really want to know I'll tell you. If you don't, skip the bit in brackets.

(A man came up to Mum and asked where she came from. Like most people. And she said Laos. He said he was Lao, and then he had a conversation about the Lao language and Mum told me to write it down, but I couldn't spell the words so the man wrote it for me.)

The man on the boat reminded me of Mr Rookes our ICT teacher, and another reminded me of Freddie Mercury.

There was this other person on the boat who was like an exact mix of Liam Trott and Glyn Hornsby. And before you ask, no I don't.

SATURDAY 11th JULY 2009

Dear Diary

I've got a new pen and Melie lost £30. We went to Canal Village and looked at lots of shops. We're not having a dress made because it's too expensive.

Sorry, I had to write postcards and massage coconut oil into Mum's feet! Yuck!

Anyway, we went out to the cafe at Canal Village and Amelia realised she didn't have her purse. We looked everywhere, so someone must have taken it. Dad got really cross, which meant he broke his promise (of not getting cross) so now he owes us £10 each.

It's raining and someone's just got married. Melie and I went with these people to play some games, it was like a PE lesson. We didn't get to go on the climbing wall, it was too wet.

Dad's ill (well kind of) my legs ache and we want room service (well I do) and to watch tele (mum's idea).

Dear Diary, It wasn't Dad snoring like an elephant, it was bullfrogs! How stupid can you get? We were trying to spot one. Trouble is we don't know what they look like.

SUNDAY 12th JULY 2009

Dear Diary

It's almost supper time.

How I feel, puzzled, (a)mazed, mad, crazy, weird.

Sorry about that. We've been at the kids' club almost all day and we made cookies and cookie boxes. My cookie box has elephants and flowers on it. I drew them myself. We just cut out the cookies and decorated them. The lady came round saying, 'Doo fad' and 'doo tin'. Scuse me a mo.

Hi I'm back. I had to undo my hair. It was in plaits. Franka and Nynka were there for the morning, we made pictures of crumpled up tissue paper. Me go have shower. Bysy byes!

Sabaideebor means hello/greeting

Khobkhunlai means thank you

Khunchui alai means what's your name?

Shandraikun means I love you

Zaep means nice

Zaplai very delicious

Laquoin means goodbye

Chokdee means good luck

Dear Diary, we are in the bar again. Mum keeps peering at you because of the Lao [above]. We met the Lao man again. I'm going to practice writing my name in Lao.

MONDAY 13th JULY 2009

Dear Diary

We are now by the swimming pool. Since when has there been deep fried ice cream?

TUESDAY 14th JULY 2009

Dear Diary

I'm here waiting for the water taxi. Melie's trying to touch her toes. Hey! She grabbed you complaining that she's hot.

I've got to do some stretches a sec. Sorry, I was demonstrating our P.E. lesson to Mum. Oh look! Here it comes!

Dear Diary, we're at the tailors now. Mum and Dad are about to have their clothes fitted. Apparently Mum's dress is a bit loose. She is standing in front of a mirror in a start shape. She looks funny. Dad is sitting staring at me and doing his annoying smiley thing. Now we're playing I spy, M is the letter, and it's my go, (It's a mirror) and Dad's given up. Melie hasn't and she's got it!

Dear Diary, it's 10 o'clock and I'm really tired.

We played with Nynka and Franka in the pool. It was really fun. We bought a lilo and a ball.

Afterwards we went onto the beach and then got changed and hung around in the lobby waiting for a shuttle bus to take us to Canal Village where we ended up eating a Mediterranean meal in an Italian restaurant and playing on a bouncy castle which was amazing (and suddenly disappeared) goodnight.

WEDNESDAY 15th JULY 2009

Dear Diary

Today:

- Dad weed in the bath
- I got stung/bitten by a black bug thing.
- We played in the pool
- Mum and I are going on a trip
- It's raining
- I forgot to take you to the pool

- I predicted that something bad is going to happen
- Our guide is here
- The Prime minister of Thailand is coming
- The elephant hugged me
- Dad filmed a lot
- Melie said 'no' a lot.

THURSDAY 16th JULY 2009

Dear Diary

We're at breakfast and guess what? We're waiting for Melie. Mum and Dad are talking about Afghanistan. Yesterday on the zip wires was really fun. Dad said he would have done it.

Franka's hair braids have come out. She and Nynka are here feeding the elephant. Mum is telling Melie to go back in and get a banana. We had breakfast in a different room because the Presidents of Asia are in our usual place. I just fed Mina (the elephant) a banana because Dad fetched some. Mum gave Nynka and Franka a banana too.

We're at the pool now.

Dear Diary Nynka and Franka have left and we're getting ready for supper. We played in the pool together and went down the slide on the lilo, but Melie wouldn't as she was too scared.

They've gone back to Australia now, but I've got their email address.

I spoke to Grandma on the phone earlier. We are now in Lulu's bar and we're going to the Tom Yam Goong place.

FRIDAY 17th JULY 2009

Dear Diary

We are waiting in the lobby of a jewellery shop.

It's part of a tour and we went to a temple and a batik painting demonstration.

We are discussing tours with the Mr Rookes person. We have decided to go on a tour to the James Bond Island and go kayaking, snorkelling and visiting the sea gypsies.

Speak to you later, we're in the car now.

Dear Diary, I've just been on a jet bike and had my hair braided. The jet bike was really fun. We're now watching tele as we get ready for supper. Pink Panther is on.

We're in the lobby and Dad is trying to get people to understand about a restaurant called 'Kargo' that we want to go to. Mum and Miels have gone to get a booklet. I'm sitting here being bored.

SATURDAY 18th JULY 2009

Dear Diary

Today we went on the 4 in 1 trip and first we went snorkelling. One time there were so many fish around me I couldn't swim. There was lots of coral and we saw Nemo. I saw Gill and Dory as well, and then we went to the James Bond Island and saw a lady that was on tour with us yesterday. On the boat we were with the Mr Rookes person again. His real name is Lek and he speaks good English. After that we went to the Sea Gypsies and had lunch there. Their whole village is on stilts above the water. Dad kept taking pictures of the people which I thought was rude. Dad wouldn't let me talk to you he said, 'Put that stupid thing away!' but you're not stupid are you?

SATURDAY 19th JULY 2009

We then went on a canoe and someone rowed for us. Me and Melie went together. Meanwhile, Dad was taking photos. Afterwards we went swimming and I got stung/bitten by something. On the way it was rather bumpy. I sat in the front.

The Mr Rookes man asked this little girl if she had a boyfriend, then he asked me, and I said, 'No, but people think I do.' Some people will say that's complete nonsense, but it's true because boys are stupid!

Dear Diary, I'm really tired. Guess what?!!?!

Melie went down the water slide!!! Dad had to carry her up the stairs and push her down the slide on his lap. They went so slowly. I went down after 10 seconds and banged into them on the way down.

Then Melie said it was too fast. Dad told her to go the waterslide with me on the lilo, but she went ahead of us as we were walking there and went down on her own.

She was then forced to go on the lilo and really enjoyed it and said, 'That's really fun! Again, again! 100 more times' (typical).

We then went on a little walk along the beach which turned out to be a very long walk in fact. I collected two shells (very beautiful ones) which someone at a restaurant cleared away. Dad took a million and one photos. We climbed on rocks, saw someone fishing, Dad weed in the sea, saw a crab chucking sand, found out the sea was really warm. Mum said that was the first meal she actually enjoyed and Melie complained that her feet hurt. What a surprise!

MONDAY 20th JULY 2009

Dear Diary

The baby sitter's here. I can't speak long I'm really tired. We went down the water slide this morning, and this afternoon. I made a banana and bacon sandwich at breakfast.

For lunch we went to the kids' club while Mum and Dad were at Patong/Batong (and still are now). We watched Wallace and Grommit. The baby sitter is watching tele, the programme sounds good even though it's in Thai. See ya!

WEDNESDAY 22nd JULY 2009

Sorry I didn't speak to you yesterday, I didn't have time. You didn't miss much. We only went on the waterslide for the very last time. I nearly drowned myself and Melie kept pulling me up again crying, then said that if I wanted to drown I could have stayed under. That's the thing you see, I don't want to drown. Or die.

We went to a different place to eat lunch and supper. We packed our bags and next day came to the airport and boarded this plane. The one we're on now. And I've watched '17 again' and now I'm bored. Goodbye forever Diary!

In loving memory of Gran died 2003/4/5? [12]

Thank you

Mum

Dad

Melie

Thai Airways

Laguna Complex

Laguna Tours

All the people in Phuket

Whom without

This

Diary wouldn't

be the

same

Thank you Thank you Goodbye

---

[12] Jemima's paternal great-grandmother died in 2003.

Granny + Morah
Jemima Layzell 2009

Tree

By Jemima Layzell age 11

Now I am old I think back on
The things I used to be
I once stood tall and proud and strong
With leaves of green hung on
The thing is now I've sunk right down
And the green leaves now are dead
The power of age has crippled me
And all my beauty gone
But I shall rise and live again
To sing my one last song.

TUESDAY 9th FEBRUARY 2010

I fainted [13]

APRIL 2010

Old is Wise

(Growing up is optional but growing old is not)

A play by Jemima Layzell

Curtains open and old ladies: Molly Ann Sue and Rosa are sitting in a living room knitting.

SUE: I need a bloody miracle.

MOLLY: I like Annie

SUE: I wish I was Annie.

ANN: Are you talking about the musical 'Annie'?

MOLLY: I like Annie.

SUE: Oh Molly, will you please shut up!

ROSA: Sue stop acting like a 5 year old you know how Molly is.

SUE: Oh for god's sake will you stop acting like my mother, she's my bloody twin sister.

ANN: How long did Annie wait for a miracle?

ROSA: Ten years.

SUE: And we've waited a bloody 62 and a half.

ROSA: And why are they covered in blood?

ANN: Rosa, why do you have to be so literal?

ROSA: She has to learn not to say that when the child is around.

SUE: Well, she's not around is she.

ROSA: Beth is only upstairs.

---

[13] This entry was in a separate big black diary and was one of the only entries.

MOLLY: I hate toenail scissors.

SUE: Why do we have to look after the horrid child anyway.

ANN: She's not horrible, she's just a bit confused. Like Molly, that's all.

MOLLY stands up and starts singing the chorus to 'It's a Hard Knock Life' and dances around the room. Everyone stares. She then sits down again.

MOLLY: I remember Harry.

SUE: Here we go again!

MOLLY: He went to war and . . .

Someone knocks on the door.

ALL: Ooooh!

Knock

ALL: Ooooh!

MOLLY: I'll get it. It might be Harry.

Knock

MOLLY: Ooooh!

ROSA: Poor thing

SUE snorts, ROSA and ANN glare at her

ANN: I just don't have the heart to tell her . . .

ROSA: To tell her . . . ?

SUE: Oh for god's sake woman.

ANN: To tell her that . . . that . . .

ROSA: Harry's dead.

ANN: Harry's dead.

ROSA: How did he die?

SUE: Oh not this . . .

ANN: I don't know, how did he die?

ROSA: Did he die?

ANN: You said he died.

ROSA: No you said he died.

ANN: But did he die?

ROSA: How come he died?

ANN: I never said he died.

ROSA: Liar.

ANN: Liar

ROSA: You're the . . .

SUE: Who's acting like blinkin' 5 year olds now!

Silence again. MOLLY finally gets to the door and opens it.

MOLLY: Harry!

ROSA: That's not Harry.

MOLLY: Oh no. He looks familiar.

MOLLY peers at him and sits down again.

MAN: Where's my Beth?

Silence

BETH: Daddy!

Curtains close

The End

Boom boom crash!

May 2010. Birthday party down by the river with Grace.

JUNE 2010

Hayley is going out with Sam. I am happy for her. You know sometimes I dream the future. I dreamt someone had asked Hayley to marry them. Oh, and I also had a dream that Nick, Jordan and Josh asked Hayley out. Odd.

Hayley and Maddy are arguing. I am not sure Bon Bon Boutique [14] will last very long.

Sunny's died. Just before Sunny (my baby rabbit) died I had a really weird feeling something was going to happen. Good or bad we were walking straight into it. I have that feeling again but slightly weaker and more on and off.

---

[14] A fundraising club selling cakes and gifts at school.

Photographs taken on holiday in Rhodes, July 2010.

FRIDAY 15th OCTOBER 2010

Dear Diary

I have just seen inside Sophie's mind. I didn't mean to, it's just, her thoughts were so strong I couldn't help it. Her mind is all a bit muddled at the mo. It's a right state in there. I won't be going inside for a while. Can't make sense of anything and it hurts. Real bad. I can see some things from where I am right now but not too clearly with all the other thoughts randomly buzzing round the room. Gotta go bye

Dear Diary, we're waiting for Mum to pick us up. We're outside. Waiting in silence for fear of being found out and sent to prep.

Oh, she's here. At last.

Right then MAdD, here we come.

SATURDAY 16th OCTOBER 2010

Dear Diary

Saturday school. Fml.[15]

Still a shock to remember
The red face in the flames
His evil laugh betrayed
The joy with which he smiled
He told me of madness
Of which I was possessed.

---

[15] Texting-speak for 'f*** my life'.

Aged 12, at her grandparents' house.

TUESDAY 28th DECEMBER 2010

My dream means (apparently):

☐ My secret hopes will be discovered but gained in the end.

☐ I will be vexed by anger

☐ I am ashamed of my ignorance (I am?) and there is a golden opportunity looming.

☐ I will discover something of great value in a surprising place.

☐ I am better at English/maths than geography

☐ I will have success by my own efforts

☐ I will soon receive a party invite

Tick the boxes if it's true - get it?

WEDNESDAY 29th DECEMBER 2010

My dream means:

☐ I will work hard to achieve my ambitions

☐ Warning: I should choose my friends carefully

☐ Warning: I will need to have all my wits about me to withstand some temptation which will be put in my way.

Tick the boxes when each one comes/is proven true.

THURSDAY 30th DECEMBER 2010

There is a golden opportunity coming and I will need to work very hard. I will experience strokes of bad luck and misfortune, I will need to have all my wits about me to withstand temptation and overcome obstacles. I will soon try to become the peacemaker between friends, most of these quarrels can be avoided if I am tactful and do not try to harm my enemies or else I will suffer. I should probably choose my friends more carefully. If I succeed in this challenge, which is most likely, I will live in ease, my fortunes will improve, my secret hopes will be discovered, but gained, and I will discover something of great value in a surprising place.

If I fail which is unlikely, but still very possible, things can only go in one direction.

Down. [16]

The Muffin Bunny Rap

I was dressed as a muffin in the middle of May

I was down by the beach when I fell in the hay!

Then the muffin bunnies came and saved the day!

I was well chuffed man it was hip hip hooray!

The rainbow ponies are like so yesterday

Yeah the frickinfrickinfrickinfrickin bunnies! Word!

---

[16] Jemima had been given a book on dream analysis for Christmas.

Mother's Day card March 2011.

APRIL 2011

Death Came Knocking [17]

Him

Death came knocking upon our door, Death and his scythe. When Death decides today is your day to die, believe me nothing in the world is going to protect you from him, nothing in the world will change his mind.

Death claimed my love as his own. He took my wife. He left me behind. If you have ever lost someone close to you, then you'll know how it feels.

If you haven't, you can't possibly imagine it, and it's not something I can begin describe. Death robbed me of the one thing I treasured, my reason for living, and I still wonder why. He left me with nothing in this world left to live for, yet somehow I live on. Time passes. It passes slowly, painfully, though it feels impossible time could still pass at all, pass it does. I remember.

When Death came knocking upon our door, Death and his scythe.

Her

Death came knocking upon our door, Death and his scythe.

I was not ready. There was all my life I had yet to live. So many things I was going to do. So many things I was going to be. I couldn't leave yet. Not here, not now. Time froze as Death had knocked, once, twice, thrice, four times. I still wasn't ready. But then I realised, there was no more life I had yet to live.

No more things I was going to do. No more things I was going to be. I was going to leave. Right here, right now. Death had decided. He required my soul, so my soul I gave.

---

[17] This was a re-working of a school piece written following study of *Weathers*, by Thomas Hardy.   This version was a birthday present for Jemima's maternal grandfather.

There are so many things I wish I had done. So many things I regret. I watch over my beloved every day. I see his antagonised face. I hear his cries. I feel his pain and his reluctance to go on. The last words we had exchanged were harsh words of hatred. Words we did not mean. Words we had spoken a few weeks before we parted. Words we wish were of tender love and care, spoken as he cradled me in his arms whispering to me endless comforts of pointless promises. They were not such words. My life had not been lived to its full. It had not been a life lived for others. They took pity on me. You may not be so lucky.

Human mortals, take moral. Your end may be near. Change your living, make amends. Live today like there's no tomorrow. Any moment may be your last. You'll never know, until Death comes knocking upon your door, Death and his scythe. . .

Idea 4 story

The Truth and its Lies

The story is told by Grace but from her family's point of view, except for the first bit which is in past tense. Grace meets a boy on the internet and thinks she is in love with him although they have never met. They decide to meet. Her parents don't allow her to go, but she sneaks out at night and is never seen again.

'Lying is like murdering the truth yet it still comes back to haunt you and the knife does cling to skin. Though when the truth comes creeping back it will not go away, you stab and stab, again and again but it only comes back stronger. The knife traps your hand around its hilt, while the blood drips for all to see. You lie down flat, the truth breaks free. You cannot run, you cannot hide. The truth may leave but it takes you with it.'

Amsterdam, April 2011.

[The mother of Jemima's friend Gracie committed suicide on 5th May 2011. She was also Jemima's mother Sophy's best friend. Polly had struggled with depression and had been diagnosed as bi-polar with occasional paranoia and delusions. Despite threatening it regularly her actual death was a great shock to everyone.]

MAY 2011

English Exam   8 R Mr Manners

Revenge is Sweet

Why should I write something just because I have been told to? Why do I need to write about revenge being sweet? Revenge is most certainly not sweet. Don't you know anything? When people write it's like God creating the world. God created us with free will. Options. Free to do as we please. That is how words should be. Free to flit and dance across the page.

REVENGE IS NOT SWEET!

That is what I say anyway. Of course the difference between my story and God's world is God supposedly has no beginning and no end. My story does of course. Although I suppose the Universe is said to have had a beginning. I wonder if it will have an end....So if God just wanted to bring the world to an end could he? Just like I could do to this story and just say stop.

But seeing as I have 10 minutes left I won't stop there. Does my story have a purpose? Does this world have a purpose? I probably won't get any marks for this and everybody else will write a lovely typical short story about somebody avenging someone else. Blah blah! But my story IS the revenge, and it is most certainly sweet. You probably won't even spot it! But it's there alright.

Weaving in and out of the sentences, peeking out of the words! Jumping out in front of your blind eyes when you aren't even looking! (If you think I'm talking about the words in pencil then you are really stupid) And I absolutely will not refuse to NOT write a story about REVENGE BEING SWEET! 'Cause it isn't . . . so there! :P [18]

SATURDAY 9th JULY 2011

Dear Diary

It is times like this when I sit and wonder 'where's my Romeo? What happened to my Prince Charming?' But then I stop and think, do I really deserve him? Diary, I have lied so many times. I have done terrible things.

But are those things really so bad? I suppose they are sins but it's not like I've murdered anyone. I should really be asleep by now, it's almost half past eleven but I need to write. Writing (and drawing) to me is not so much a want. . . it's more like a need, even though my hand aches, my eyes strain, my head throbs, I need to write.

---

[18] Emoticon for sticking your tongue out.

I want to leap out of bed, draw back the curtains and gaze out into the night. To lean out the window, sing for my true love, the love I do not yet possess and possibly never will. If only I weren't so afraid.

Aged 13 at her Year 8 Prom, 11th JUNE 2011.

Outside something is there nothing?

What is nothing

What is something?

Has there always been something?

Before there was something was there nothing?

Why did it stop being nothing?

Why did it become something?

Did the something just spring from nothing?

Why am I here?

Why are you here?

Do we have a purpose?

What if we don't?

Has the something just been here forever?

With no beginning?

Will it go on forever?

With no end?

Did God create something?

Could he turn the something into nothing?

Could he give the something an end?

And just say

STOP

SATURDAY 9th JULY 2011

Dear Diary

I have tried to sleep but I can't. Every time I try to close my eyes they seem to always pop open again!

I don't understand how I can be so tired but unable to sleep! No matter, I shall try again! Gracie is round for a sleepover and snoring like a pig! I can imagine her laughing while reading this and laughing at my stupidity! I can't help feeling someone's watching me, but of course that can't be true. I can't decide if I should be scared by the thought of it, but can't help being fascinated at the idea. I am going to be shattered in the morning. When my eyes get tired, (like they are now) I often get a really big blind spot just up and left from where I am looking. It's hard to describe though. It's not black. It's not white. It's certainly not in between. It's just nothing, a big fat nothing in the middle (ish) of my vision.

I kinda wish Gracie was awake, that she'd talk to me.

Or that the boy of my dreams, the love of my life, would climb in through my window and hold me till the darkness crept away. Then again I should be careful what I wish for. I mean a complete stranger breaking in through my window in the middle of the night probably isn't such a good idea!

When I'm older I probably won't be able to read what I've written. I'll be looking back on it and thinking OMG WTF was I trying to write??

Anyway my bad handwriting is due to the fact I can't really see, I'm really tired and my hand is shaking so bad I have to keep hitting them [it] to stop them [it] from going into spasm. Whether the shaking is from fear or just fatigue I don't know, but I should start seriously thinking about actually getting some sleep now! Wish me luck!

'To become a wise man you must first play the fool.'

Dear Diary, yes it is still 9th July. I have not slept and it is 0:46. Grace is starting to scare me a bit. She keeps rolling about and doing weird things with her breathing, she seems like she's chewing on something that isn't there, she sits up and opens her eyes and starts talking but falls asleep as suddenly as she woke! I sometimes begin to wonder if she's actually asleep.

But I think she definitely is. Oh! Romeo, Romeo! Wherefore art thou Romeo! I still cannot sleep!!

My head is just full of ideas! Buzzing with questions, answers, new ways of looking at the world! My thoughts are full of possibilities, impossibilities and everything that is, has been and is yet to come. Who's to say what is impossible anyway? Any man who thinks he can is a fool!!!

SUNDAY 10th JULY

Dear Diary

I have much less inspiration to write than I did last night. My brain is far too tired. Grace has gone, it's just me now. Sitting on my window sill, staring up at the sun filled sky.

Wishing I belonged up there, up in the clouds, soaring with the birds, flying high above the roof tops. No one would laugh at me then. But no, I'm sitting alone in my room trying to imagine somewhere else I could be right now! Somewhere that didn't hurt. The dogs are barking next door again. I miss our dogs. Tamoo and Kabisa. Yes their names are a bit strange, but laugh and I will honestly murder you! We have our cat Tilly and our rabbits.

Here is a timeline:

Kabisa born

Tamoo born

Tamoo died

Tilly born

Kabisa died

Sunny born

Jack born

Sunny died

Poppy born

I can't remember the dates, the lifelines are only estimates and when I say 'born' I mean when we got them, my dearest Poopsie [Poppy] for example we got when she was 1. Sunny and Jack were both bought at the same time. Sunny died within a month. We came down one day and she was just lying there. I wondered if she was sick. I picked her up. She was all stiff. The life sucked out of her. Right then I felt like joining her. I kept blaming myself, I was convinced it was all my fault. I cried for hours just thinking of all the good times we were going to have together. All the moments we were going to share. It seems like only yesterday I was watching her hopping across the lawn, leaping in the bushes, climbing up on my chest and licking my face. Poppy needs me now. I must love her for all eternity, 'We are 3 gorgeous girls', I often say to Tilly poos, 'You me and Poopsie pie!' Aren't we just!

SUNDAY 10th JULY

OMG! I have just shaved off all my pubic hair. Yes I do regret it slightly but I am glad I did it. It feels so free! . . . and slightly exposed. . . anyway we are going to Egypt on Tuesday so we are starting to pack and stuff.

MONDAY 11th JULY

Dear Diary

Egypt tomorrow! So excited! At least, I think I am.

I seem to be getting less and less excited by things. Last year Christmas didn't feel like Christmas and even my birthday wasn't nearly so exciting. At Christmas I usually wake up at like 2 in the morning running round the house shouting and jumping on the beds. It wasn't anything like that last year.

I lay in till about 8.30 and my sister had to practically drag me out of bed!

I'm really bored.

I'm gonna go app shopping. Byee! I'll write later! Promise XD [19]

TUESDAY 12th JULY 2011

Dear Diary

It is so HOT! I am lying here sweating in my bed. But it is AWESOME!! You can practically taste the air. It tastes of kinda sweet spices! We have a separate room from Mum and Dad (thank God! No offence but his snoring, well, think of the worst snoring you've ever heard, times that by ten and you're almost there! No kidding!) We arrived at night and it was all lit up, it looked so magical! We have a balcony overlooking the pool. I honestly think I could sit there all day.

I just can't shake the feeling something really bad is going to happen.

TUESDAY 12 JULY 2011

Dear Diary

I'm still lying here. I've been thinking about what I want to be when I'm older. I used to want to be a princess or a spy! Then I began to think more realistically and wanted to be an artist. Then an architect (before I lost interest in buildings) now I would quite like to be an author and rather fancy the idea of being a fashion designer although that will probably never happen. But I guess I just don't know yet.

You see I don't care for flashy cars, or expensive jewellery. I have no interest in designer clothes or magazines and heavy makeup. I won't be drinking and gossiping in some bar, hanging out with some guys who I actually don't know, totally obsessed with money and sex. I don't care what others may say.

---

[19] Emoticon representing a face grinning.

I have no interest in what they do behind my back. I won't be crying in some corner because of it.

But I guess I don't know yet.

You see, I want to be happy, to be free, to be loved and to just be me . . .

SATURDAY 16th JULY 2011

You know the sun isn't the only thing that's HOT here . . . I've seen several really fit guys, most of them aren't English though. There is one exceptionally gorguss [*sic*] boy, but I'm not sure what nationality he is yet. He has a younger sister who is also very pretty. I've only seen him once so far though. There's a foreign one who keeps appearing everywhere, he has done something to his right leg, it's in a bandage. I feel quite sorry for him, on holiday not being able to do anything while he watches his many siblings play.

I wonder if my Diary would be worth anything in the future.

OMG. He is. Beautiful! Did he just look at me? OMG he looked at me, he actually looked at me!!

Oh shut up Jemima! He's probs taken bacon anywayz . . .

MONDAY 18th JULY 2011

Dear Diary

I can't believe we've been here for almost a week. The hours tick by so slowly and the days go zooming past. Hang on Brb! [20] Just talked to Grandma on the phone. Diving tomozzies! I don't really feel like writing today, so I'm going to read my book! Sozzicles, Byee!!

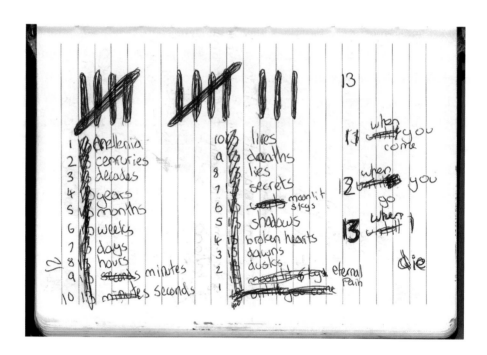

TUESDAY 19th JULY 2011

Dear Diary

Diving was soo cool! But it hurt like hell! Seriously, my ears! And oh my God that guy with the leg was there too.

The bandage was off and it was just a cut.

---

[20] 'Be right back!'

He's a bit too good to be true tbh.[21] Right now we're watching Pearl Harbour in our room. We're going to the restaurant Italiano tonight.

We saw loads of dolphins! There were about 20 of them swimming by the boat! It was BEAUTIFUL, such show offs though! You can't describe it, it's heavenly.

Dear Diary, I just want to make it very clear that I do not fancy any of these boys here! OK! I just think they're kinda good looking! Ok now bye!

Jemima and her father.

---

[21] 'To be honest'.

Jemima and Amelia.

FRIDAY 22nd JULY 2011

Dear Diary,

I am so bored!! I feel soo ill!! I haven't eaten in ages. I've gotten rather thin, which would be a good thing if it weren't for the fact that half my bras no longer fit me and the pathetically tiny bit of cleavage that I did have is now gone! Anyway I've got diarrhoea it is gross! It's all green and runny and also means I can't really go anywhere (extremely annoying) so I might not be able to go to Cairo tomoz to see the pyramids ☹ I had to have an injection which I suppose was ok. He took my blood pressure which was the bit that hurt. He kept pumping loads of air into the thing I thought my arm was going to fall off! But apparently I had low blood pressure and I have no idea what that means. In fact I'm not really sure what blood pressure is.

But Dad says low blood pressure is bad, even worse than high blood pressure (not sure what that is either but presumably the opposite of low blood pressure).

The doctor seemed to be able to know I had an infection in my tummy just by pressing it! And then he said I was really dehydrated so I was put on a drip!

I was looking at the wall so I didn't see anything. I just felt a really cold chill spread through my body from the inside of my elbow on my right arm.

I didn't even know what was happening, next thing I knew there was a big long tube sticking out of my arm! Big Shock! And then I had to go to the loo half way through so we had to carry the drip thing with me. He turned it off and my blood went up the tube, so he had to take the tube off the thing sticking in my arm and all the blood went EVERYWHERE!

I had to try and think of happy stuff to distract myself but it turned into sad stuff. I thought of home but then I just wanted to go there.

I wanted Sunny back. I thought of her with Jack, Poppy, Tilly, Tamoo and Kabisa, all of them playing in our garden together.

Do you think there is such a place as heaven? I hope there is, and that Sunny, Tamoo and Kabisa are happy there. I'm sure we'll meet again.

I end up crying because of it and looking like an idiot so I tried thinking of people worse off than me which just made me even more depressed, so I settled on thinking about chocolate.

The doctor was a good one once he actually came. We spent 2 HOURS waiting for him! On the notice it said he was open at 11 so that's when we went there, but after half an hour he wasn't there so mum and dad went to find out what had happened to him and apparently the time was changed to 12, so we saw no point in going all the way back again, so we waited . . . and waited . . . and at 12.30 we were told he wouldn't be there until 1 o'clock 'cause he was praying!!

By this time Dad was getting very cross and no longer wanted to play I spy. It was very hot but I stayed calm and waited patiently, as they say, 'Patience is a virtue', not sure what a virtue is, but it sounds positive. Goodnight!

SUNDAY 24th JULY 2011

Dear Diary

OK the good news is_ I'm alive and on holiday ☺☺

The bad news is_ I have to take these tablets that get stuck in your mouth ☹

The good news is_ they work ☺

The bad news is_ I didn't go to Cairo yesterday ☹☹

The very good news is_ that's because we're going tomorrow ☺☺☺

The extremely bad news is_ Melie might not be able to go ☹☹☹

The worst news is_ Dad might cancel it completely ☹☹☹☹☹

SUNDAY 24th JULY 2011 [again]

Either I'm going mad, or it's some side effect from those pills. I had all these visions. I told Mum they were dreams but they weren't. It was as though I was there. A bit like it was happening right in front of me and a bit like a memory.

I'm not sure if it is something that had happened, was happening, or is going to happen.

At first I was watching the scene. It was all black, then it was so bright! Fire everywhere! I saw two girls in the fire. I do not remember exactly how they looked, only that they were young and scared. I became the older one. I could hear her thoughts. She was so like me. She was me. I was her. But she was different. In a way I can't describe. It may have been me, but it isn't this me, the one who's writing right now.

The girl was her sister, our house was on fire! No alarms sounded, we were trying to wake our parents . . . but they slept. We couldn't do anything to wake them up. They just lay there. Not even breathing. I had to drag my screaming sister away. It was so hot. There was no air.

And my sister . . . she was too late to come through the door out the bedroom and the door frame was soon ablaze. I told her, 'just step through', but she didn't she wouldn't. She begged us not to leave her but we did. The fire closed in around her, she burst into flames. She screamed and screamed.

I wanted to tell her I loved her, but the words stuck in my throat.

Her face, her face was on fire. And her eyes, they saw everything. They burned, and then were gone.

She turned on her dying sister and she fled. She left her! I left her . . . why would we do that, diary?

Why did we leave? Why didn't we go back? Surely there was something we could have done! She died Diary! And it was ALL OUR FAULT!

Outside they waited for me, they came after me, they hunted me down, they followed me, they chased me, they trapped me, they killed me. I won't make you listen to the details. It was horrible. They made me watch others die, until I told them. Until I answered their question, I didn't even know the question, let alone the answer. It was awful Diary! I can't stand to even think about it.

SUNDAY 7th AUGUST 2011

Dear Diary

Why is everything so complicated?

Yeah I know it's been centuries since I last wrote, blah, blah, blah! I'm sorry, I've just been . . . busy. I don't want to go through the bore of writing down everything that's happened since then, what was it? — 24th July. 24th July? . . . that was yonks ago!

Anyway I need to write what I think and feel. Not all that you see here actually 'happened' but it's still very real to me. I don't care if I let my imagination run away with me! Plenty of brilliant artists and writers were mad! In fact it made their work more interesting!

Even if they did cut their ears off, commit suicide, run round doing crazy stuff etc etc. People still loved them and their work just the same. And I want to be loved too.

I almost feel as though I will never live long enough to become an author, to be married and have a family.

Then again nothing bad happened on holiday, so I probably will.

I should probably mention I rode a camel, you know just in case I look back on this and think I'm going insane 'cause I swore I rode a camel but I don't mention it kinda thing.

Hmmmm . . . I wonder if it will be love at first sight, or I'll spend ages searching for the one when he was right there in front of me, or maybe I'll never find him at all. Or I will, and then I lose him and never see him again, or he'll only come into my life when I'm old and grey and practically on death's door, but even that won't matter, at least I'd have him. Whoever he is. He'll be worth the wait.

MONDAY 8th AUGUST 2011

Dear Diary

The world seems to have lost its colour. The sun does not shine so bright. Its heavenly rays do not feel so warm upon my back. It's like nature's lost its beauty. Of course, it hasn't, it's just me not seeing it. Why do I not see it anymore? It's as though now I'm 13 a door has been closed in my mind. I am so desperately trying to open the door but I can't find the key and each time I think I'm close, they change the locks!

Some people say that God can't exist because if he did he would help all the poor people in the world.

I object to that. I feel their despair but WE have to help them. They are there because we did this to them. They are there because we have a wrong to right. They are there to stop us from turning into complete monsters before it's too late.

A Play

H, P and Jemima are changing to go swimming.

H: hey new girl what's your name?

P: I'm Phoebe.

H: Cool! You need to have a shower now. Stupid school regulations. It's just through there . . .

Jemima: Except it might not be!

H: *(ignoring her)* Oh and unless you want to be called a lessy perv for the rest of your life, do NOT look at the populars dancing in their underwear!

P: OK . . . *(hurries off head down)*

Enter S

S: Where did Phoebe go?

H: To the shower

Jemima: To the shower that might not be there . . .

S: Oh shut up Mima of course it's there!

Jemima: But how do you know it's there? You don't!

H: Yes we do! Cause I've just been in there. Doh! Keep up!

Jemima: But...

H: Fail Mima!

Jemima pauses for a moment to compose herself.

Jemima: No . . . You're the fail. Your failing is to open your mind to all the possibilities of this world. *(Trying to stay calm)*

H rolls her eyes and walks towards the swimming pool door.

Jemima: You're not listening to me! *(Very angry that she's always pushed around in other people's shadows)*

H: Look around you! No one is . . .

Jemima: No YOU look!

H: I'm looking!

Jemima: No you're not! You're barely opening your eyes and even if you were looking you're certainly not seeing!

H: *(sigh)* Same thing . . .

Jemima: No it's not.

H: Alright stress!

Jemima: I'm not stressed! How could I possibly be stressy, when I know that I am right and you are wrong! Besides wanna see stress? Take a look at yourself once in a while.

H: *(through her teeth)* What's your point?

Jemima: My point is that no one knows what is and what isn't! Nothing's impossible! Now if you'll excuse me I have a swimming gala to win!

(J smiles and waves to S as she slips through the door)

P enters

P: Umm . . . I can't find the shower . . .

The End

What a strange feeling it is to poo. You probably don't want me to talk about it. I don't see why poo is considered rude. It's just a poo! Jesus pooed! It is a strange sensation. How sometimes it gets stuck half way, how sometimes it hurts, and other times it falls straight out in a mushy liquid. I don't see why people are so disgusted by it. Well girls and adults are anyway. Some of the boys aren't but then again they themselves are disgusting. Most of them, not all of them. But let's not talk about Boys AGAIN!

As you can probably guess I'm on the loo. I'm in the downstairs loo at Grandma's. My book that I'm reading is called 'Red Riding Hood'.[22] It's actually better than I thought it would be, it says something I found really interesting: 'How strange it is to have a sister, someone you might have been . . .' I've never thought about it like that before.

Do you reckon I'll ever make it? You know, become a bestselling author whose books are loved for decades. I suppose I'll have to stand out, to do something different and special, and to do it well.

WEDNESDAY 14th AUGUST 2011

Dear Diary

I am planning to come to school in year 9 a new and improved me. So I need to practice talking!

---

[22] By Sarah Blakley-Cartwright & David Leslie Johnson.

Which may sound strange but I only ever really talk to my family and my girlfriends. I wanna be that person all the time. I'll get practice on the 20th as Wendy has invited me, Phoebe, Harry and Salvi into town for the day so I can talk to them, get my confidence back.

Another plan of mine is to get my parents to buy the box set of FRIENDS! [23] I love FRIENDS! I really wanna buy all of them 'cause we keep seeing them in the wrong order and missing some out. So I am being extra nice and helpful, then I'm going to ask if I can buy it. It's £39 from Amazon, and I know that's a lot but I'm willing to pay that much 'cause I have been saving and saving and this is what I really want, and if Dad buys it from Amazon with his account ('cause I don't have one) then I can pay him. And yes, I have thought about this and yes, I am sure. And it's my own money, surely I can do what I like with it and I'll still have £10 after I buy it and that I love them and please, please, please can I buy it?

I don't know the main storyline and each time I watch an episode I have to ask myself a load of questions like are Monica and Chandler married? Is Rachel pregnant? Wait! I thought Phoebe knew who her Dad was? I thought Monica and Chandler couldn't conceive, why are they trying? So I'm basically watching for the laughs. And Friends is one of those things you can watch over and over again and you will never stop laughing!

THURSDAY 11th AUGUST 2011

Dear Diary

Oh how I wish I had some exciting news to tell you, but me being me and my life being so boring barely anything exciting happens to me. Oh I do miss the good old days of 7P. When we were young and wild and free!

---

[23] The hit US sitcom series.

SATURDAY 13th AUGUST 2011

Dear Diary

I'm always doing something wrong. I really do try to be helpful and kind but it never goes right. I'm useless. Good for nothing. It seems like all I have is my art, and you Diary. Well, I could just lie here and wallow in self pity or I could quit moping and get some sleep so I can be the bouncy optimistic person I am longing to be. Enough with the superstitious nonsense and freakishly strange weirdness! I shall push it all away and then let it all bounce back again when I write. Ooooh wait, is that Grandma? Code red! Lights out! Stations!

MONDAY 15th AUGUST 2011

Dear Diary

Why does my soul feel so sad? Why does my heart feel so glad?

To love or be loved? That is the question!

But I cannot help but feel, that, if love being as special and as dear as it is, the magic that makes the world go round, is it too much to ask for both?

No, I am not in love with someone nor is someone in love with me. I am just in love with the idea of love and how I want love so!

TUESDAY 16th AUGUST 2011

Dear Diary

Today at MAdD we were writing some of our own music, so I went home and wrote some of my own.

Dear Diary

I know I probably shouldn't be up right now. I just get so happy in the day and so sad at night. Is that because I'm tired, is the happiness just a mask, or am I just really stupid? I don't know why I am being so negative. Usually, I am really optimistic. It's like, I spend half my time telling people how beautiful life is, but at the moment I'm not even convincing myself.

You can just see Jemima's black and white nails from the show.

SATURDAY 20th AUGUST 2011

Dear Diary

The performance [24] went really well. Thomas actually painted his toenails pink!

You see me, Charlotte, Eloise, Katie, Sophie and Thomas were all 'peach buddies'! We all painted our toenails like a rainbow 'cause of when we all huddle together to make the centre of the peach.

We ran out of colours so I painted mine black and white. It was so cool!! In fact I am still wearing it now.

Me and Eloise got married as Lily and Jacob and then we went on our honeymoon to Venice and climbed the tower to the fortress of love which later became the fortress of Lepricorns [*sic*] aka lesbians! Lol! And me and Eloise pretended to snog to try and freak the boys out and stop them attacking. It didn't work. It did the exact opposite! I'm just trying to write it all down so I don't forget it. It's 23:11 I actually shouldn't be up but tomoz it's Dad's birthday and he has Kat, Dan, Celia, Matt and Ellie (who 'gate-crashed' the party) they're so loud talking about all that dodgy stuff. They can't seriously think we can't hear them?! The conversation kinda generally creeps back to 'le penis' :/ lol [25] XD it's funny listening to them, and kinda depressing cause if they knew half the things I say and do . . .

SUNDAY 21st AUGUST 2011

Dear Diary

I gave Dad an etching of a jelly fish I did at school for his birthday! I am so proud of it, we got it framed and everything!

---

[24] A MAdD holiday workshop where students put together their own interpretation of *James and the Giant Peach* by Roald Dahl.

[25] :/ indicates a rueful face, Lol means 'laugh out loud'.

OMG I am so excited about Saturday I could scream! I just feel so . . . ALIVE! I feel brilliant, spectacular! Like I could do anything!

It's 10:30 and I don't feel at all tired. We've just watched 'Son of Rambow' and I want to cry it was so moving! I just cannot wait till Saturday! The sleepover with Wendy has moved to next week instead of this week!

It's gonna be me, Sock,[26] Phob, Wendy, Harry and Salvi! The boys aren't coming to the sleepover obvs! But imagine if they did . . . ok Jemima . . . too far! Honestly, if someone read this Diary I think I would die! Just thinking about all my girlfriends, boyfriends and all the fun we're gonna have, sends a thrilling sensation up and down my spine! I have a feeling something amazingly exciting is going to happen tomorrow! I really want it to, but hey, let's not get our hopes up too much!! I'm going to sleep now! Good night!!!

I LOVE MY LIFE

TUESDAY 23rd AUGUST 2011

Dear Diary

You know I had a feeling that yesterday something exciting was going to happen, well it did! I got my ears pierced and it did not hurt! Only £8 as well!! I am a very happy bunny and I've written lyrics to one of my songs (with some help from my lesbian wife Eloise) I call it . . . The Choice! And I've made a score using my FREE computer programme musescore! It's brilliant!

The Choice

'I have a choice and I cannot choose

And either way I will only lose

Why should I have the final say

I'd rather die than choose and pay

What happened to the world of Christ our Lord

What we have done is of our own accord

Just you and me now we're in this together

---

[26] Sophie.

I choose love and I'll love you forever

I have chosen, I have no regrets

I guess I knew from the moment we met

The fiery pits of hell we no longer sail towards

Our secrets lie safe in my heart they are stored.'

Do you like it? We also made up these 'awkward' things you know like 'awkward turtle' [27] and stuff, so far we like best:

Awkward balloon (pretend to blow up the balloon, tie it and then hold it up by your face with a really cheesey smile. We didn't technically create this one, but we still love it!)

Awkward banana (have the imaginary banana by your ear like a phone, take it away, peel it, eat it, do over exaggerated chewing and swallowing and then freeze looking at the banana with head cocked to one side)

Awkward umbrella (pick up the umbrella, pop it open, stand under it and then shiver like you're really cold.)

Awkward lesbian (this one's kinda rude but also very funny! Warning not to be performed in adult company! Hold your forefinger and middle; like swearing and hold it up to your mouth, stick your tongue through and pretend to lick! Gross right? But trust me, it's hilarious to share with girlfriends! Just saying the words 'awkward lesbian' cracks us up!)

FRIDAY 26th AUGUST 2011

Dear Diary

I'm at Grandma's house. It smells so wonderful here in the airing cupboard. I used to sit here all the time when I was little.

---

[27] A hand gesture, originating from the US, which is supposed to break the spell of embarrassing moments.

It's just so peaceful. Somewhere no one can disturb me and I can have some time to myself. I used to sit here with Melie and play games and stuff, it used to be our 'secret hideout' and the challenge was to sneak downstairs get cushions blankets and food without being discovered! It was fun. I like to just lie here like the rest of the world no longer exists.

Here is the story of Lily and Jacob

The two lay under the peaceful night's sky, gazing out over the ocean and into the stars. You could tell just by the look in their eyes how much he loved her and she loved him. Lily was one of those girls who never really talk but somehow say everything. She was a very pretty girl with long curly golden red hair, green eyes and lips that natural pink colour that most girls would kill for. She didn't care for it though. All she wanted was Jacob. Jacob was every girl's dream.

Need I say more? And there they are, side by side, and neither of them would change that for the world.

'Wow! A shooting star!' Lily exclaimed as she bolted upright. It had always been one of Lily's dreams to see a shooting star. And this one took her breath away. It was so much more beautiful than she had imagined. She felt as if it was made just for them. Jacob sat up too and hugged her.

'Make a wish Lily' His body was so warm against hers. It felt superfect,[28] as though it was always meant to be there, and there it would stay. She concentrated on her wish, let it fill her up, become her. She begged to the moon, to the stars and the sea. And she . . .

'So . . . what did you wish for?'

Lily sighed, 'I can't tell you that! It won't come true'

---

[28] A word of Jemima's own, meaning 'super-perfect'.

'It might' Jacob grinned. He didn't really know what he was grinning at, but he did anyway. That's just Jacob.

'You don't even know what I wished for, and . . .'

'True' he cut her off, 'but I know you.'

Jacob's mysterious like that. Lily edged closer.

'So tell me how much you love me?' she asked, confident in the answer. Jacob thought about this one for a moment before replying:

'I can't.' Lily was baffled. Did this mean he didn't love her? She was nearly in tears, but Jacob saw how confused she was and finished his statement.

'I can't tell you, because words are not enough. They cannot describe the love I have for you.' Lily smiled, tears of joy trickling down her freckled cheek,

'Then show me.'

So he got down on one knee and pulled out a ring. A ring so beautiful even the goddess Aphrodite herself would have been jealous. Lily gasped. It was the most wonderful thing she had ever seen, besides Jacob of course.

'I . . . I don't know what to say!' She didn't know what she had expected. Whatever it was, it wasn't this. But this was so much better,

'Say yes!' he pleaded, 'Lily Parkinson, will you marry me?'

'Yes!' she flung herself into his arms, 'Yes I will ' He slipped the ring onto her delicate finger, as they kissed on the edge of the sea.

'Jacob,' she whispered in his ear, 'my wish came true.'

They gazed lovingly into each other's eyes for a few moments, before turning back to look at the stars once more . . .

THE END

SUNDAY 28th AUGUST 2011

Dear Diary

My friends really like my Lily and Jacob story!

I like it too. I keep reading it and getting all emotional. My plan worked by the way! I don't think I've ever talked so much! I feel confident buying stuff and talking to adults etc. Be right back, I'm going to have a nap.

Lol. It was so fun! I stole Harry's wallet and left him in the lift! Got to go now byeee!!

WEDNESDAY 31st AUGUST 2011

Dear Diary

Life is fascinating. Not sure if that's in a bad way or a good way. Maybe it's both. Why is everyone so stressed all the time? Why am I so stressed?

There is nothing to be stressed about. I suddenly just feel so angry. It feels like I'm dreaming, like I'm really far away from this place, in another dimension, trying to wake up. Perhaps that's all that life is, a silly dream. How do I know that what I think just happened, really did? I don't! But I can't go on living my life like that now can I? Oh what happened to the days when everything was all laughter and games! When we didn't care about boys or makeup! Where the biggest disaster that ever happened was that my pencil fell down the drain!

The First Draft

Although you are covered in cheese, do not disturb the pickle pot with your army of dancing gherkins.

I see the flowers the trees, the clear blue sky. I smell the fresh morning air. I feel the sun on my back and the cool breeze blowing my hair, and I feel alive. So peaceful. So in harmony with the rest of the world. I want to stay here in this moment till the end of time.

Mum

I did not have a chance to say goodbye

I said some words I really had not meant

I told her that I hated her and went

What have I done, I've made my mother cry

How to avoid avoiding the unavoidably avoidable.

How I just wish it would all go away

For I am left behind while she's moved on

You never know what you have till it's gone.

I'm walking but I don't go anywhere

My destination gets further away

The darkness do I enter do I dare?

MONDAY 5th SEPTEMBER 2011

I really don't know what to write, but I suppose I must write something so I shall just write as I think. Celia my Godmother says to write every morning when I get up. She's writing a book you know. I want to be an author when I'm older and maybe a part time art teacher or something. I like to think of myself living with my family and my cats in a cottage by the sea, a few acres of land, a river running by with great willows at its banks. But all I want is to be happy, to be free, to be loved and to just be me! That probably sounds really cheesey!

I'm so glad I'm in a class with Phoebe! Even though we don't talk that much she's still one of my best friends. The senior school is really scary! I mean, they're all so big!

SATURDAY 10th SEPTEMBER 2011

I actually really like school! So glad tomorrow's Sunday though. I'm just finding it really hard to focus on what I'm meant to be doing right now. I mean I'm meant to be writing about stuff that's happened right? Although no one ever said I have to write that. It's my diary, it's my life, I can write what I like!

SATURDAY 24th SEPEMBER 2011

I'm so glad Grace is here, well not here here, but she's at my house, she stayed over last night and she's staying tonight as well. I haven't seen her in ages. She seems pretty sad, delayed shock I think. She was always so happy, laughing, playing, lighting up the world. I miss her even now. I think about her all the time. And it hurts so, so much.

MONDAY 26th SEPTEMBER 2011

Dear Diary

I'm sorry we haven't spoken or such a long time.

School, well, it's school, but senior school is so much better than the prep school. There is just so much more freedom! Everyone says that but it really is true. A lot more responsibility as well though, like if you're late for a lesson you get a detention and stuff. Yh, but it's ok I guess. There's a really nice new girl called Florence, or flo-rida as she likes to put it! ♥ my friends but I feel they are somehow distant. I keep going from feeling extremely happy to so, so sad! I can't control it and I can't stop it. I cry and cry, half the time I'm not even sure why, but I laugh at the pain and smile through the tears. I have to. Grace came round this weekend. I miss her. Even when she was right there beside me I missed her. Because she wasn't there, not really.

She says it's like she's falling down a deep dark hole, and no matter how hard she tries, she just can't get out. She's not the same since Polly committed suicide; she always used to be so bubbly, bouncy and happy.

She used to fill the room with light just by walking in. She just seems so empty now. But I need her. She's my best friend in the whole wide world and I love her so much. The worst part is that they never even got to say goodbye.

SATURDAY 8th OCTOBER 2011

Do you reckon it's normal to hear voices and see faces? I mean, other than ones that belong to a person. It's not really like hearing voices, more like seeing voices and hearing faces. That probably doesn't make any sense to you at all. And I can't eat. It hurts inside, deep inside. And then I hurt for hurting, because I don't have the right to be upset about losing something that wasn't ever mine.

I don't like writing about the 'real world' anymore, because this world doesn't seem real to me, not since . . . anyway it doesn't matter, not to you.

I can no longer tell the difference anyway, between what's real and what's not.

There's not even breathing room between joy and pain. Maybe they're one, maybe they're the same.

Maybe there's no line separating the lies and the truth, between dreams and reality. I just don't know what to do anymore. So all I can do is just cry.

Sophie, Jemima and Flo at school.

Chicago 1981

That was the first night I dreamt of him. He came for me, I waited for him, he held me till the darkness crept away. He told me he was dreaming too and we promised to find each other, I will never stop searching, not ever, not for one second.

73 (my favourite number)

THURSDAY 13th OCTOBER 2011

I know you are real

I know I love you

I know you love me

I will find you

I'm coming,

Just like I promised.

I believe

I believe in you

In me

In us

Forever.

Where are you?

I'm trying to find you

But the more I try and remember

The more I forget.

I'm coming.

I love you

That much I am sure

But I have no idea who you are

Or if we'll meet again.

Oh, where do I start!

I can't remember what you look like,

What you smell like

What you sound like,

And I can't remember your name.

All I have now is your hand in mine,

Your breath on my neck,

And your arm around my waist,

And the belief that you are real,

We are real

And we shall find each other once more.

I'll keep searching, I will never stop.

Not for one second.

I promise.

SATURDAY 15th OCTOBER 2011

Dear Diary

Halloween!

I'm pretty sure I've spelt that wrong! But it looks kinda cool!

It's nowhere near Halloween yet but Mrs Cutts is going on about it in an English lesson. She's letting me write 'cos I've finished my book. Oh wow! I forgot it's Saturday! You see what happens when you give children too much prep! They forget what day it is and how old they are!

Wednesday night I dreamt of him. He came to me, I chose him, and he held me and comforted me. He made me feel safe and loved. I met him walking along a path and I heard fair music, so I went into the park. He was there. We jumped from roundabout to roundabout. He walked me home and said goodbye.

I thought I was never going to see him again, but he became one of those gap student teacher work experience whatever you call 'em things at my school and all my teachers always came to me saying that he never spoke of anything but me! I remember seeing him again had made me feel happier than I'd ever felt in years! I was older than I am now. I went round to his house and he offered me a glass of milk which honestly looked a lot more like cream, but I can't drink milk! We went out to a coffee shop and well this is embarrassing! I dunno if I should write what happened next in case some nosy whatnot decides to read it! But yeah I was what 14/15 and I think he was 18ish. I thought we were just friends, but that wasn't how he saw it! I hope I can remember what happened next 'cos I'm too scared to write it down!!

Anyway by the end of the dream we were back in his house on his couch and I was sure I loved him too. I didn't know I was dreaming, it was like I was in a separate world and this one didn't exist, but as we curled up on the sofa I suddenly realised I was dreaming. I told him this but he said that he was dreaming. So we promised to come and find each other in this world, so that is what I'm trying to do.

THURSDAY 20th OCTOBER 2011

The Somme

This place is filled with such outstanding natural beauty. The leaves seem to glow, speckled with the dazzling rays of the sun. But it wasn't always this way. Once there was nothing. Once there was pain, sadness and death, fear of everything. Even now you can feel the saddening horror hidden behind the peace.

Where I lie
This is where I will lie
This is where I will die
This is where I will drown
I'll be boiling in my blood
I'll be screaming through the flood
I won't have a chance to say goodbye
There will be no one left to hear my cries
She loves me
And I love her
But now all that's left is hurt

This is where I now lie
This is where I now die
This is where I now drown
I am boiling in my blood
I am screaming through the flood
I don't have a chance to say goodbye
There's no one left to hear my cries
She loves me
And I love her
But now all that's left is hurt

This is where I did lie
This is where I did die
This is where I did drown
I was boiling in my blood
I was screaming through the flood
I didn't have a chance to say goodbye
There's no one left to hear my cries

She loves me

And I love her

But now all that's left is hurt.

Picture taken by Andrew Jolley (History tutor).

Reflections on the first half of term

Top three moments
- Dancing to 'All that Jazz' with Eloise XD
- Sleepover with my best friend in the whole wide world
- Washing up with Phoebe ☺ and people

Plans for Half Term
Me and my friends and I are going to 'revamp' old clothes and model them at a fashion show to raise money for charity.

Top Three Targets
- Keep on top of that humungous pile of prep!
- Commendations ;)
- Be happy

SATURDAY 5th NOVEMBER 2011

Wow I totally forgot we just came back from half term! Feels like we've been here forever. I've recently been drawing lots of mermaids, some pictures are peaceful and happy but most of them are dying chained on the floor. Everyone says I'm really disturbed and to put some clothes on them, but they don't understand that it is just how I can express myself, I feel so much better afterwards, like I've released all my emotions onto the page. It's a bit like how I feel after writing or composing, or dancing, except it comes more naturally to me, it's more free, and I don't care what anyone else thinks of it.

THURSDAY 17th NOVEMBER 2011

I'm sorry I can't it hurts the voices too bad too much can't think can't hear they speak strange things always there talking why she left I don't know help me make the voices stop they scream they shout they don't make sense words thoughts faces everywhere the fire burns the clock ticks voices what's happening if he'd loved her would she still be here would she have jumped I'm sorry I can't concentrate too many voices please make them stop why do I see the faces why does no one else help me so confused I feel trapped inside someone else I don't expect anyone to understand how can they when even I don't understand oh no what have I done

See Appendix for an explanation of this.

SATURDAY 19th NOVEMBER 2011

I can't believe it. I never knew people could be so mean. Judging me on the lies that others told. Now they all think I'm completely insane. I didn't really do anything.
 I don't know how much they think they know- but I just hope they don't know about the voices.

SATURDAY 26th NOVEMBER 2011

I'm going to visit Gracie tomorrow. She's in Exeter Hospital.[29]

SATURDAY 3rd DECEMBER 2011

Gracie's out of hospital. I hope she'll be ok. I'm so scared. I feel so far away. Like I'm looking in a mirror seeing a reflection of a world I thought I lived in, but I can never really be there.

---

[29] Grace was admitted to hospital for anorexia.

WEDNESDAY 7th DECEMBER 2011

I was in the changing room, I don't remember why.

'Look there she is, poor thing!' I heard someone say mockingly behind me. I turned around expecting to see the other girls coming to jeer at me again, but there was no one.

The voices, I realised.

They began to laugh at me, buzzing around my head,

'He doesn't actually exist! You did realise that didn't you?'

'Such a weird, stupid girl,'

'Worthless scum.'

'She thinks she can hear voices.'

At that the voices all laughed. And they just continued to say stuff. Lots of stuff I couldn't make out. Getting louder and louder, full of disgust and . . .

'Stop!' I yelled inside my head. 'Go away, and leave me alone!'

For a moment they died down until I heard a snigger from beside me. A cry of pain from above, I ran to the mirror about to smash it when they all said,

'A little stressy are we?'

I cried as they laughed. I wanted to destroy everything. Everything, everyone . . . especially me. My eyes turned to the hockey stick across the floor in front of me. If only it was sharp.

'Go on.' The voices whispered, 'You know you want to!' And I did want to. I felt I deserved only pain, and to suffer. I wanted to spill my own blood so badly and then I felt so ashamed. The voices laughed again. I threw it down. Ran to the loo with the book clutched to my chest. I locked the cubicle door behind me, curled up in a ball and waited to die.

A Story

Dear Diary

I thought I was getting over him, over his death. But he came to me again last night. We went back to where I found him. We went back into my dreams. He was there like he always is, like he always used to be, in our meadow whispering softly to my sleep.

I know nobody ever believed me when I told them we first met in a dream, but I know it's true, and so did he. We promised to find each other. I said I would never stop searching till I found him. And I did find him, only to lose him again.

"I love you." He always says to me.

"No," I reply, "No you don't. If you did then why did you do this to me? If you really loved me; you wouldn't have jumped."

The dreams seem to last a life time, they're always the same. Over and over, time and time again. It's driving me crazy! I'm not sure if I can stand it much longer. But part of me yearns for more, to fall back into sleep and be with him again.

The dreams are all I have left of him now, and I want it even though I know all too well how the story ends. It's as though too much is somehow not enough. I want to go back and get it right, I promise myself that next time will be different . . . but it never is.

I still don't understand why he did what he did. Even as I stood on the edge of the cliff beside him begging him to stay, he just kissed my forehead and took another step towards the edge.

"No" I had pleaded screwing my eyes up tight "please don't go. You promised you'd never leave me."

"I know" he whispered, taking his hand in mine "but I was never really there."

I remember opening my eyes about to ask him what he meant, but he was gone.

I never felt his hand leave mine, and sometimes I swear I can still feel him, like he's right there beside me. Thing is, it seems he didn't just die that day, he suddenly never existed and only I remember him.

She closed her battered, old diary. It was late, dark, and her throbbing head was so confused she couldn't even remember her own name. Turning back towards Amelia she realised just how late it was, and laughed.

"Melie shouldn't you . . ." But her sister wasn't sitting on the bed as she had been a few moments ago. Strange, Melie had gone to bed hours ago. How had she forgotten?

"Wow, I guess I really must be going mad!" She half-heartedly joked to herself, collapsing on her bed with a sigh.

Having been the bubbly, enthusiastic girl everyone knew and adored people just couldn't understand how she had become so empty, almost overnight.

Katy . . . Kate. Katy! Katy? Yes, that was what people called her. Her name. Katy? Wake up Katy!

Please Katy, wake up . . . Not giving a single thought as to what the voices were or where they were coming from, Katy closed her eyes to drift into sleep.

A sleep probably a bit too deep. A sleep she was already in and had been for a very long time.

Katy jerked violently in her sleep, muttering strange words as her mind floated through the valleys they used to walk. Then she saw him.

"Is this real? Or is it all just in my head?" Katy asked. It always started like this, but he never used to reply.

"Of course it's all in your head! But why should that mean it isn't real?"

She was about to tease him for quoting Harry Potter, but when he slipped his arms around her waist it hit her. The whole world suddenly came rushing back, crashing down upon her like a wave against the cliffs. What had happened to the world in which she lived? A world that in just a few short moments she had already forgotten.

"I . . . who? What? Where am I? This isn't happening. I don't understand . . ." Katy stammered, completely dazed. It had never happened like this before. She panicked.

"Shhhh. You do remember? Don't you, Katy." He asked, smiling. But it wasn't a question.

"I do remember" she found herself saying, unable to tear her gaze from his dark, shining eyes. Her mind involuntary flashed through images of her floating away from her lifeless body on the cliffs. He had led her like he'd walked this way a thousand times, but she fell.

Everything was turning from unreal to surreal. She was so desperate for answers she would believe anything that was thrown at her.

I am nowhere. I am half way. I have run round in circles with no idea where I was or where I was going. I have run from the person I was trying to run towards. I am here half way between here and there, right and wrong, good and evil, love and hate. Half way between all and nothing, now and then, heaven and earth.

Please Katy! Come on sweetheart, you can make it!

I had never left the cliff. The past year never happened.

I'm in a world that doesn't exist.

Katy. Katy! Stay with me Katy! Katy!

I can hear my parents' cries beside my crumpled body. I am half way between life and death, drowning in my tears, not knowing how to wake up.

The countless thoughts invaded her head. She knew deep down they did not belong to her, but she did not care. She convinced herself it was the truth.

He had died long ago and she wanted to die too, she wanted him to kill her. She wanted him to tear away her soul and rip her body apart. She wanted to kiss him as they cried tears of passion, screaming, sinking down to hell.

"Take me with you"

Grinning, he led Katy by the hand, and she willingly followed him to her doom. She gasped in horror as she stood in the gateway of a hell he'd made for her, but it was too late. With a scream, she was gone, and the gates closed shut . . .

Making a birthday present for Granny.

Christmas 2012, drinking non-alcoholic champagne.

SUNDAY 1st JANUARY 2012

The Boy with Burning Lungs

I awoke one night, in quite a fright

To find a boy at the foot of my bed.

He stared surprised, with ghostly eyes,

And in a pain filled voice he said:

'Please help me sir, this world is a blur,

There's no oxygen reaching my head.

No air to be breathing, lungs screaming

Drowning in blood I have bled.'

The scene was insane, I felt his pain.

Capillaries nearly all dead.

Blood stopped pumping, head stopped thumping,

And burning, this boy's life was shred.

He held out one hand, crumbled like sand,

And from his soul then had fled.

Whatever happens next I want you to know that I love you. I'm sorry that it has to be this way. So cold. So hungry. It hurts.

I so want a baby. More than almost anything I've ever wanted. Oh crap, I guess that means I need a guy! But I'm serious. All I want in my life is to fall in love, have children and become an author, and Gracie of course, I want us to be best friends forever, I wish for her only the best. Thing is I feel so ready to have a baby. Not physically or financially, but mentally. I feel if I was pregnant right now, my world would be complete.

THURSDAY 4th JANUARY 2012

I wonder how Gracie is doing in hospital. This just isn't fair. She deserves the world and I would give it to her if I could. None of this world is fair.

Why do I sit here with so much when other people out there suffer? What have they done to deserve that?

And me, I'm just a spoiled stupid little girl wallowing in self-pity over stupid little things! I'm nothing special, though I spent many a night pretending I was, wishing, hoping. It's time to wake up out of your precious little bubble. This is the world I thought I lived in, the life I thought I knew. Don't be so pathetic, 'In life you are presented with two paths – the easy and the hard, each has its rewards, but with the easy path the only reward is that it's easy.' I guess dying would be the easy path, finding happiness the hard. Maybe not for everyone, but for me. But I'll keep going. Love must exist, and I will find it. Somewhere, somehow . . .

My eye keeps suddenly twitching! Annoying! It's really weird. I don't know what to feel anymore, I just feel so empty. I dunno why, cause it's not like anything majorly bad has actually happened to me. Grace is doing really well now she's moved to St George's hospital. She says she's finally getting the help she needs which is really good and everyone is really nice, they gave her a really nice welcome with banners and everything, she has met a girl from Taunton school there who also has anorexia, but I wish Gracie wasn't so far away. I mean she's all the way up in London, which I guess isn't as far away as it could be but it's not all that easy to visit her.

TUESDAY 17th JANUARY 2012

Dear Diary

Yesterday, coming home from school had to be THE best car journey I have had in ages.

It probably won't sound particularly great but those few moments sent a thrilling chill up and down my spine, and my heart pounded with pure excitement.

I had this wonderful feeling I just can't describe, when I saw he was actually looking at me!

I don't know the guy but he was pretty fit and sitting in the back seat of the car, him and a friend, I couldn't see the driver. I was sitting in the back (Melie's turn in the front) when his car pulled up next to ours in a traffic jam and I saw his incredibly sexy grin press up against his window.

He stared right at me and I was so surprised and shocked and looked away quickly, pulling down my skirt before staring back. He then raised his eye brows as if to say, 'how about it then?!' On the spur of the moment I smiled and licked my teeth. OMG I didn't realise how stupid that sounds. It felt a lot better at the time. Well anyway, his grin widened at that. He was clearly a lot older than me and didn't think I was just a measley 13 years old. He pointed to himself, made a heart with his hands, and pointed at me.

I managed to stifle a laugh and turned it into a silent giggle, I mean I couldn't let my mum hear, but our car pulled away and I blew a kiss to the guy I would never see again. It was just a bit of fun really. And it felt EPIC!!! L☺L

WEDNESDAY 18th JANUARY 2012

Dear Diary

I had such a sad dream last night. We were driving along the motorway. I started to daydream staring blindly at the verge and then suddenly we were spinning wildly. Mum managed to gain some control so that we were facing forwards but there were a couple of tipped up cars in front of us.

'Look out!' I cried to my parents in front, but it was too late. I managed to throw my door open and leap for the edge just before our car crashed.

I fell into a hedge full of thorns. Grasping, I plucked them from the palm of my hand and looked up to see a boy kneeling beside me. He must have been a few years older than me and he was staring at me with such sympathy I wanted to cry. He stood up and held out his hand to help me up, I took it, standing up slowly.

'Thank you,' I said quickly before whipping my head back round to the car.

Our car was almost completely crushed.

My parents were trapped inside our car but my sister was crumpled in a heap in the middle of the road. I held my breath, please God don't let her be dead, please don't let her be dead. She shook as she tried to stand, her hands covered in blood. She looked to me and just stood there. Her eyes seemed to stare at me with such knowledge and understanding that saw past this world and its lies. She looked right through me and the car hurtling her way. She never even glanced at it.

'Melie! No!' I screamed as the car slammed straight into her body, and I screamed and screamed and screamed. Even when I closed my lips the screaming did not stop. And I just stood there. I don't know for how long. It could have been seconds, hours, days, weeks, years. I just stood there and watched the world burn. I couldn't hear anything. The whole world turned silent.

Mum, twisted and trapped, helplessly shook Dad's blood covered lifeless body, before she saw the fire. She closed her eyes and prayed.

'Get down!' said the boy beside me, I couldn't hear him, I didn't realise he was still there, and I wasn't responding,

'Please get down!' he said again. Then my brain started working again,

'Mum!' I tried to run, but he held me back. He grabbed my arm so tight I thought it was going to fall off.

'No I won't let you, this whole thing's gonna blow!'

'But that's my Mum in there!'

The earth shook and blew up, scattering into a thousand pieces. I stopped struggling. The boy pushed me down just in time, his body on top of mine protecting me as red hot sparks showered on top of us. The whole world turned hot and black. For a minute I thought I was dead, I wished I was. But I wasn't, so I just curled up and cried.

FRIDAY 20th JANUARY 2012

Dear Diary

I had such a wonderful dream. I don't remember much apart from feeling just so wonderfully happy. I was looking down and there was this beautiful baby girl in my arms. She reached up with her little baby hand to touch my face. She couldn't quite reach so I bent down so that she was touching my nose and she lit up with pure joy.

'Mama!' She squealed with delight. She wrapped her hand round my finger so tight and I knew I couldn't possibly love anything more.

SATURDAY 21st JANUARY 2012

Dear Diary

This morning I was about to perform the usual bore of dragging myself out of bed at 6.30am, I had the strangest feeling. I could sense a presence. I sat very still on the side of my bed, staring at the wardrobe, not daring to move an inch. The feeling moved in a cluster and turned to sit beside me on my right, watching me. I couldn't see it, I couldn't look, but it was there all right. It put a hand round me and onto my left shoulder, and I knew that it was Polly, I just knew. It wasn't scary or anything like I would expect it to be, but it was kinda sad and peaceful. She stroked my hair and I turned to face her, but everything dispersed and floated away as if it was never there. But it was, I felt it, I know I did. She was there.

SATURDAY 21st JANUARY 2012 [AGAIN]

Hi, you know that dream where the car crashes and I'm left screaming on the verge watching the whole world burn before my eyes. Yh, well, I keep having it over and over, each one more vivid and tragic than the last.

Gosh I just read through this book and realised how depressing it is! I'm not depressed or anything, so why can't I write happy stuff? I dunno, but whenever I write a happy story it doesn't sound right. Even when I just write the classic 'Once upon a time there was a girl held captive by an evil witch, then the hero, Prince Charming rescues her. He defeats the witch and they live happily ever after. THE End.' Maybe it's because there's no such thing as a happy ending? It's just a story and in real life it just wouldn't happen. I mean everything in life ends in death, how is that happy?! Unless perhaps dying is a release from this single formed human life full of pointless pain? I dunno, don't care.

Maybe I should, maybe I do. Why is everything so confusing? I wish I was either a young innocent child, or a mature adult, I hate all this . . . stuff, in-between. It's stupid, like can't God have created a simpler method of reproduction, that perhaps didn't involve bleeding every month and having all these strange disturbing unwanted attractions and feelings and images invading my head?! Uurrgggghhh! Anyway got to go to ICT bye.

Heyy I'm back! It's like 1.45 and I'm just sitting in Besley all by my lonesome little self, waiting for Mum to finish work. Lessons finished aages ago and I've been doing all the prep I can do without a computer while eating sherbert lemons. In fact I'm going to have another brb! ☺

Eeeek I only have 4 left. I am so bad at paragraphing, especially when I'm just scribbling like I am now. It's 5 to 2 Mum should be here soon. Celia gave me this notebook and I have decorated it with pics of me and Gracie, Ali and Melie and she's given me this book called, 'The Right to Write,' and It's AMAZING!

OK. I've made up these characters. There's Kitty (f) Alex (m) and Ross (m). Ross and Kitty are brother and sister, Kitty is really stubborn towards Alex as he always makes fun of her but actually really likes her. They end up developing a romantic relationship which Ross finds slightly annoying and disturbing but strangely cute. They are fugitives running from Government spies having been trained by some elite force for an experiment without their knowing.

Kitty 14

With these big blue eyes and bouncy blonde curls you would think she was some innocent girly 16 year old, you couldn't be more wrong. This girl can manipulate almost anyone to do almost anything. She isn't all that strong or good at fighting, so she has a knife which is always tied to a belt around her hip (hidden of course) and knows self-defence and stuff. She's clever (at what she knows) and lucky for her she's fast. Oh, and she couldn't care less about her looks. She's amazing!

Ross 17

Pretty much thinks he's the leader as he's the oldest, but he isn't really (he's not all that bright, bless him) but he's really strong, the best fighter, so brave, loyal and protective of his little sister. He doesn't know much but what he does know he knows well, like how to kill a grown man with one punch etc. He is super cool! With his dark hair and six pack, girls swoon at the sight of him.

Alex 16

The brains of the group. He knows pretty much all there is to know about breaking and hacking into stuff. He could shoot someone straight in the head about a mile away. He's not as strong as Ross, he is taller and slimmer and has light brown shaggy hair.

He comes up with most of the plans, is a quick thinker and super observant. He and Ross joke around together a lot. He knows all about survival and what to do in different situations as well as all the medical stuff. He's awesome!

I'm not sure what to do about the name Ross, I always think of Ross from friends. I think I might call him Jack, but Mum says that Ross makes him sound more interesting. You know I think I will call him Jack.

You know I think I will write a book about Alex, Kitty and Jack. I'll do it on the computer 'cause it's easier to change things and stuff. OK, so I have the characters, next op – the Plot. Hmmmm . . . I dunno. So let me see. They are running from the government (stuff like MI5) and have been trained by a secret elite force which they escaped from and they are on the run.

TUESDAY 24th JANUARY 2012

Where am I? Who am I? I know I'm Jemima Layzell, 13 years old. I live in Horton, go to Taunton School. I have a little sister called Amelia, my friends call me Mima etc. But who is that? Who is that? Who is Jemima Layzell and what am I doing here? Who am I really? I'll meditate on it.

WEDNESDAY 25th JANUARY 2012

What the hell am I going to do when I'm 18 and still have never had a boyfriend. I'm going to die a virgin! Oh God! I'm going to be one of those single old ladies who grumble about on those walking sticks, waving it at kids who knock on my door and run away for a joke! Oh gosh I am actually going to be one of them.

Hi I am now sitting in the changing room. It's been a while since I heard the voices, hopefully they won't come back. Ever.

I would be in Besley but it's far too noisy and I considered going to the library, but I can't be bothered to walk there, too many people and everyone else has gone to the ICT suite.

My handwriting is so messy. It. Is. Embarrassing! I'll go and get my phone so I can see what time it is. Brb!

SATURDAY 28th JANUARY 2012

NO! No No No No

Ok I feel a lot better now. I don't know why I was so angry. There's nothing to be angry about. Ok there's a lot to be angry about. But not for me. I have everything. Am I being greedy? Or selfish? Ha, ha sounds like shellfish! I really need to work on my handwriting. I guess that book's right. I mean it says: 'Being in the mood to write, like being in the mood to make love, is a luxury that isn't necessary in a long term relationship. Just as the first caress can lead to a change of heart, the first sentence however tentative and awkward, can lead to a desire to go just a little further.'

Yh she compares it to having sex which is a bit umm . . . disturbing? Weird? I dunno, but I guess it's true. I started off not really in the mood to write but after a few words everything flowed onto the page and I just want to keep writing.

SATURDAY 4th FEBRUARY 2012

Prologue

They won't notice. They need the numbers. No you idiot! You're a bloody 14 year old girl! What the hell are you doing? Get out. You can't chicken out now. You have to do this. Revenge is sweet.

I left my thoughts to argue with themselves while I took a deep breath and stepped towards the desk.

'Name?' Barked the officer buried in his papers. Stay calm. Stick to the plan.

'William Marshall Pott. I live on the farm down the road.' I lied, trying to make my voice deep and gruff.

'Age?'

'18.' Crap, that was squeaky. Did he buy it? Oh please God, please! Don't trash my life again.

The guy behind the desk looked doubtful but sighed and said,

'Thank you William Pott for signing up. Meet us back here at the square this time next week. We shall then depart for the training camp.'

Oh my God. I did it. I'm in. Ha! Boy that officer must be thick, or desperate or maybe he doesn't give a shit. Probs all three. Anyway he has given me my ticket to freedom, so whatever it was I love him for it.

Finally, my days of crying in a corner while I let a son of a bitch ruin my life, are over. This is the new me. New, improved and training for war.

I swear to God he will pay, he will pay for what he did to us and nothing is going to stop me, not now, not ever. Watch out you raping bastard, my name is Kitty Grace and I'm going for the kill.

FRIDAY 10th FEBRUARY 2012

Dear Diary

I am fed up of my life being ruled by grief. I am going to be what I want to be, do what I want to do, I am going to live. And I shall start by listing 100 things I love in no particular order.

1.   My mum
2.   My dad
3.   My sister
4.   Grandma and Papa
5.   Granny and Tony
6.   Sock [Sophie]
7.   Phob [Phoebe]

8. Wendy
9. Alice
10. Vicky
11. Flo
12. Frankie
13. Gracie
14. Queen
15. Aerosmith
16. Roses
17. Mika
18. Singing
19. Dancing
20. Writing
21. Climbing trees
22. Texting
23. Laughing
24. Watching FRIENDS
25. Pencils
26. Chocolate
27. Mascara
28. Feeling pretty
29. Making a fool of myself
30. Drawing
31. Daisy chains
32. Lily pads
33. Tilly [cat]
34. MAdD
35. Watching films
36. Hot chocolates
37. Roasting marshmallows on the fire

38. Bubble baths
39. Passing notes in class
40. Butterflies
41. Trees
42. Bubbles
43. Dogs
44. Rabbits
45. Feathers
46. My skinny jeans
47. Hanging out in Besley
48. The Dump
49. Grandma's garden
50. Sugar
51. Not having eczema
52. Just Dance
53. Mario Cart
54. Super Mario brothers
55. Sending random emails
56. Sunbathing
57. Going to the beach
58. Fish and chips on the Cobb
59. Campfires
60. Camping in Cornwall with G and A
61. Ali Pali
62. Polly's laugh (cringy but funny)
63. Coral
64. Raindrops
65. Love hearts
66. Magic
67. The sea

68.   Finding shells on the beach

69.   Being honest

70.   Nature

71.   Classical music

72.   Camellias

73.   Justice etc

74.   Elephants

75.   Cool breeze on a summers day

76.   The Caribbean

77.   Spelling stuff right

78.   Puddles

79.   Reflections of sun/moon in water

80.   Red

81.   Stars

82.   The moon (over the sea especially)

83.   Sunset

84.   Sunrise

85.   Pasta

86.   Pizza

87.   Dancing to the Time warp

88.   Swimming

89.   Archery

90.   Rifle shooting

91.   Blue skies

92.   Reading

93.   Ribbons

94.   Sparkles

95.   Asking questions

96.   Seeing the world

97.   Greek mythology

EPILOGUE

Everywhere I look is empty. Nothing feels right, but then again it isn't exactly wrong. Everything happens for a reason. It must do, otherwise, what's the point? Without you two nothing will ever be the same again. You have taken the time from my tide, the fish from my chips, the salt from my pepper, the hit from my miss. And that doesn't even make any sense. Your deaths would have killed me if I wasn't already dead inside.

'Everyone I love has been taken away from me. Everyone but Maddy and even she is distant, even she thinks I'm crazy, just like everyone else does. Maybe I am, I don't know. Isn't it nice where you are with Mum and Dad? They're in there too you know, sharing the same soil, under the same old tree.

I stand here beside your grave, wondering if I will ever be the same again. I don't know what to do anymore now you are gone.

I lay the white peonies upon their grave and I knew that they were listening. All of them.

'Goodbye brother Alex and thank you for everything. I will see you again one day.'

'Kitty', Maddy is calling me I have to go, but I will come back.

'Just not yet brother like gladiator said in the film we used to watch. Not yet, not yet. You will wait for me won't you? There will come a time where I will be beside you all under the old oak tree.'

Another 100 things I love

1. White peonies
2. Cheese
3. Autumn leaves
4. Grandma's garden
5. My fluffy cushion
6. Snuggling in bed with Melie
7. Mashing strawberries
8. Wearing flowers in my hair
9. Snow
10. Letters
11. Romance
12. Purple
13. Blue
14. Comedies
15. Philosophy
16. Bungee trampolining
17. Trampolining
18. Sock's garden
19. Sock's hayloft and Dutch barn
20. Having long silky hair
21. Pearls
22. Silver
23. Platinum
24. Pretty beads
25. Dangly earrings
26. Small rings
27. The idea of marriage and children
28. School

29.   Castles

30.   Stained glass

31.   PJs

32.   Watercolours

33.   Interesting shapes

34.   Blue skies

35.   Cake

36.   Sherbert lemons

37.   Swirls

38.   Stripes

39.   Fields

40.   Holly

41.   Ivy

42.   Bon Jovi (lol)

43.   Facebooking (sad as it is)

44.   Knowing stuff

45.   Just thinking

46.   Jacket potato cheese and beans

47.   Black ('cos it is not depressing, it is smart, sophisticated +sexy)

48.   Ice

49.   The sound of ice shattering on ice

50.   Music

51.   Art

52.   Dance

53.   Drama (I guess)

54.   Colours

55.   Eyes

56.   Smoothies

57.   Bells

58.   The Med

59. Balconies
60. Ivory
61. Egyptian cotton
62. Silk
63. Dresses
64. Embroidery

WEDNESDAY 15th FEBRUARY 2012

Dear Diary

I feel SO ANGRY and I don't know why which definitely makes it worse.

65. Cashmere
66. Palm trees
67. Coconut water
68. Golden beaches
69. White beaches
70. Lolly pops
71. Birds
72. Dolphins
73. The number 73 + hymn 73 (lord of the dance)
74. Sunlight
75. Lips
76. Feeding my rabbits dandelions
77. Watching Jack run round and leap in the air
78. Horses
79. Dogs
80. Crystals
81. Balloons
82. The idea of moving somewhere like Venice/NY or Barbados or Canada
83. Ice creams on a hot day

84.   A cool breeze
85.   Leaves dancing in the wind
86.   Ice
87.   Clear skies
88.   Underwater seascapes
89.   Oaks
90.   Splashing water
91.   Necklaces
92.   Sunlight
93.   Fresh air
94.   Fire
95.   Running though fields
96.   Playing make believe
97.   Letting my emotions out
98.   Punching stuff when I'm angry
99.   Sitting on my window sill
100.   Answering to bird calls

201. The fascinating things in life
202. Being me and not caring about a damn thing anyone thinks about me.

TUESDAY 21st FEBRUARY 2012

Dear Diary

Mum's birthday is on the 8th and she's having a party inviting everyone she knows. Melie's in charge of cake and pudding and I'm in charge of canapés and waitressing and hopefully Ali and Phob are helping.

SATURDAY 25th FEBRUARY 2012

Dear Diary

I am having a dilemma. I am trying to write my Alex, Jack and Kitty story for a short story competition but it might be too long and everything I write sounds really cheesy, like I'm trying to throw a ball really far and I think it's going well, it goes up in the air but then just falls to the ground, it's pathetic. And frustrating.

I've decided not to care what people think but it's really hard. I keep telling myself, 'If they knew what I've been through,' but in actual fact I really haven't been through anything. I'm pathetic and that's frustrating too.

I keep thinking about the future and doing something spontaneous, crazy and unpredictable, but if I plan and think about it it's not exactly spontaneous, crazy or unpredictable. I'm thinking of sailing round Europe with Gracie in our gap year and then moving with some friends to live in a city like New York or London or something for some time before settling down in the country somewhere with a family of my own, being an author and always being best friends with Gracie, Ali and Melie. Funny all their names end with an 'ee' sound, Gracieee, Alieee, Melieee and then Jemima. Only thing is, this is all going to cost a lot of money.

A lot of jumping back and forth between different subjects there. I guess that's how thoughts flow. My handwriting is getting messier and messier as I try to keep up.

Ha ha lol we gatecrashed the year 5 & 6 disco last night after madd it was really funny. They all think I'm a loser for being friends with people younger than me. I don't think I am, but then again I wouldn't know. I mean I am a loser, maybe not for that reason. That doesn't make sense does it, anyhow I can't decide what I really want in life because all the 'thinks' I think I want to fade into the background and become irrelevant to my life.

I guess I want to be happy. Doesn't everyone? But what brings happiness, love? Friendship? Money? Power? Stuff? Nature? I don't know maybe it's a balance between them all. A balance, in the middle, maybe a bit like the Buddhist middle way.

The world in perfect harmony.

FRIDAY 2nd MARCH 2012

10 objects in my immediate environment and my associations with them:

1.   A model of a skeleton with a skull that looks too small compared to its chest. Reminds me of Pirates of the Caribbean and the skeleton in Mr Williams' lab.

2.   An old fashioned tele reminds me of that doctor who episode with that woman who sucked out all their faces.

3.   The lights on the ceiling remind me of depressing over clean places.

4.   My pen I'm writing with I associate with my Dad in his office 'cos he always writes with one of these PILOT pens.

5.   The pattern on Sock's pencil case always reminds me of her and Treacle.[14]

6.   The necklace I wear always reminds me of Grace because she has the other half.

7.   There is a machine in the corner I have no clue what it does but it looks a bit like Wall-e from this angle.

8.   Hera's charm bracelet reminds me of Wendy because I bought her one for her birthday in Primark.

9.   The book 'Unwind' that Salvi is reading reminds me how the seemingly innocent can be quite disturbing. I associate the book with this horror author who came to talk to us.

10.   A load of pencils in a pencil pot remind me of Ashill when I went round exclaiming my joyous phrase, 'What a lovely pencil pot!'

The most important things to me about an apartment in L/NY

- Enough bedrooms and space
- Near park
- Near underground
- Balcony with nice views
- Nice interior and exterior
- Friendly, interesting, exciting area

Chapter 1

"Kitty, you don't have to do this. You can't leave me I'm your brother. Besides you can't look after yourself you're only 12."

"No I'm 13 and fully capable of taking care of myself. Anyway I've already told you to come too." I jumped down from the branch of the oak I was swinging on to land in front of him. "Jack," I sighed, "don't you see? Finally, I can avenge our parents' death. My days of being just a silly little girl crying in a silly little corner are over.

"I'm fed up of stupid adults telling me what I can and cannot do. Them and their 'do as I say and not as I do'. I'm taking my life into my own hands and now I am going to do something with it, something . . . something worthwhile.

"I swear to God, Jack, he will pay; he will pay for what he did to us. And nothing is going to stop me. Not now, not ever." I held out my hand, "Are you with me?"

"Kitty please . . ."

"Are you with me?"

Kissing my forehead he took my hand, "I'm with you."

And so we walked away from everything we had ever known and loved. And together, we stood on the edge, and together, we jumped.

Chapter 2

I awoke with a start.

Ok, so it's cold, dark and damp, my head hurts from where they threw me against the wall, I haven't eaten in two days and my period, which hurts like hell by the way, is leaking through my trackies and onto the dirty, stone floor.

Looking on the bright side, at least it blends in with the rest of the blood splattered all over me and the cell. And I was actually beginning to like my fit cell mate, until of course he tried snogging my chest.

Besides, things could be worse; I mean there could be spiders or something.

"Kitty, that's a nasty lot of blood you got yourself there, what happened?" I can't decide what's more annoying about that guy. The way he doesn't stop asking questions, or the fact that he refuses to answer any of mine.

I mean I've only known him since yesterday evening (or whenever it was I got kidnapped and chucked in here. I have no idea how long it's been. When you're locked up in the dark all day and night you tend to lose concept of time) but he is really starting to get on my nerves.

Oh, and his name is Alex, I think.

"Fuck off, since when did you care?" I spat, glaring at him, but I quickly looked away. Perhaps I shouldn't be so rude.

"You sure have a sharp tongue for someone so young." He smiled to himself "And hey it rhymes. I'm a poet and don't I know it."

No, you're a complete twat of a 16 year old boy who is seriously up his own bum hole. I decided to continue scowling at him. Not that it affected him much, he just grinned back.

Funny, it's been almost a year since my parents were killed, which really isn't that long, and yet it seems like the whole of my life has been this past year. I have changed so much between then and now I don't even remember who I was, the 'me' who existed before any of this happened. All the memories I have of my parents and everything, it feels as if they belong to someone else.

It's weird, this whole thing is weird, but I have yet to feel something, anything, but I feel nothing. And deep down that scares me, but I don't care. I think the not caring is what scares me the most, 'cause that either means I'm a heartless monster, or I'm like a bomb, ticking, waiting to explode.

"Kitty," He said drawing closer until he was sitting beside me, and I let him in. Don't ask me why, but I did.

I turned to look into his dreamy, hazel eyes, which were staring straight back at me. It was the first time I had looked at him properly, and he was beautiful, he really was.

"I wonder," He whispered before stroking my hair, "what secrets lie behind these golden curls," he reached up to touch my cheek, "these stubborn little freckled cheeks, those big green eyes, and . . . and those rose, red lips . . ."

He was leaning in close to me, closer and closer, he was just inches away. I could feel his breath on my neck. And suddenly, everything went dark.

Chapter 3

My whole world had gone up in flames, and I was going to burn.

Alex and my brother lay dying on the floor, shot by a man, a man who killed my parents, a man who we hunted for two and a half years, a man who now had my knife cutting slowly through his throat.

I saw my reflection in a shattered piece of glass, I no longer recognised myself.

Driven by rage, I stabbed him again and again and again and again.

One for every memory I could think of that he had not destroyed.

I was four sitting on the fence while mum gave me a jam sandwich and stroked my hair.

Stab . . .

Christmas, we were all sitting round the tree with marshmallows on an open fire.

Stab . . .

I was climbing the oak tree in our garden, Jack and I made a swing that dangled from a branch.

Stab . . .

Gracie and I promised to be best friends forever, no matter what happened.

Stab . . .

Mum and dad were talking as I lay in bed, just talking, thinking I was asleep. They hugged me and rocked me gently like there was nothing that mattered more in the whole entire world.

Stab . . .

Alex and Jack remembered each other from primary and we all become best friends over a packet of crisps in the wood.

Stab . . .

I slowly find myself falling in love with Alex, and he takes me back to the oak tree and he kisses me, not in the drunken way he did when we first met, but tender, respectful and full of beauty.

I stabbed and I stabbed until I was shaking, I dropped my knife and let it clatter to the ground. Alex was staring at me, not quite dead, not yet.

I lay down and brushed my lips against his. "Forgive me Alex . . ."

Epilogue

"Everywhere I look is empty. Without you nothing will ever be the same. Now, I've lost everything. Your deaths would have killed me if I wasn't already dead inside. I stand here beside your grave, wondering what the hell I'm going to do now, now that you are gone."

I lay the peonies upon their grave and I knew that they were listening, all four of them: Mum, Dad, Jack and Alex.

"Goodbye. And thank you. Thank you for everything. I will see you all again soon. One day I will lie beside you all, sharing the same old soil, beneath the same old stone, under the old oak tree."

SATURDAY 3rd MARCH 2012

I am in my second (and last) study period of this week. The boys have just walked in from the ICT suite. You can definitely see the social separations in the room. Every single clock in the school looks exactly the same but this one has a more silvery rim rather than a white one. A minute ago when I looked through the window the sun was shining with such warmth and brightness everything lit up and glowed. The grass looked so green, the flowers looked so happy, the buildings looked wonderful despite some of them being horrendously ugly. Hee, hee, there's a man running and he looks really funny. But now it all looks dull and I notice that the tree branches are cut off so abruptly, the windows, roofs the doors and walls of the building don't go and everything feels, very, very cold.

Five things I think it would be interesting to write about:

1. The world from the eyes of a mad person
2. The journey of something like a feather and all the things it sees.
3. School life jazzed up a bit.
4. Dreams
5. Reflections

Just for future reference.

Do you think I'm at all lessie? I mean I can never picture myself with another woman because I dunno whenever I day dream about a romance involving me it's always with a guy but whenever I think of that thing dangling between their legs I just want to throw up. Us girls, we are sexy. I see a guy and think, wow, he's hot, but the waist down just puts me off completely, I mean they have hairy weird shaped legs, the chest and arms can be nice but it's mainly the eyes, face and the hair.

With us girls everything is amazing, our hair, our eyes, our faces, our necks, our chest our arms, our abs, our hips, our nails, everything. Do you think that's why they say sex is more enjoyable for the male or are they just naturally born in every culture with the upper hand. But I can tell you one thing, I am so bloody glad I'm a girl. ☺

MONDAY 5th MARCH 2012

Dear Diary

Tomorrow is a fancy dress quiz thing . . .

TUESDAY 6th MARCH 2012

Dear Diary

I'm sitting out the RE video in the library 'cos I'm 'uncomfortable with the subject of suicide and self-harm'. I want to punch them when they joke about things like that.

I don't know if I'm going to the quiz any more. Wendy bailed, Acton's ill and it's well past Salvi's bedtime! So now I have no one to go with. I didn't place in the short story competition like I was hoping. Josh won and I can't remember who the runners up were. Today could have been one of the best days in the world but so far it's just full of disappointments. I guess whatever happens I'll just be the weird girl in the corner.

WEDNESDAY 9th MARCH 2012

It was my mum's birthday yesterday. Dad paid for a kindle which I gave to her. Lol ok that is such a boring few sentences. I feel really uninspired. I feel like I should write her a story or draw her a picture or something. I'll read my book a minute and maybe I'll be inspired.

WOW that's weird I feel so much better. Like I'm un-damming a river and letting the valley flood. When I get let out I'm going to visit places in school and simply write.

I'm focusing

SATURDAY 10th MARCH 2012

Jemima collapsed and was rushed to Musgrove Park Hospital in Taunton, Somerset. She was then transferred to Frenchay Hospital, Bristol where they operated to remove a giant dissecting aneurism.

SUNDAY 11th MARCH 2012

She was transferred to Bristol Children's Hospital.

TUESDAY 13th MARCH 2012, posted on Jemima's Facebook page:

Your always in my thoughts and forever in my heart ♥ memories have just been flooding back and i just really want you to know what a wonderful friend you are and how much you mean to me ♥ trying to think of more to say, you deserve every kind word there is, but I can't list them all, like I can't list all the times you've made me laugh, or bought a smile across my face. Wishing you the best and sending you all the love and hugs i have to my Pengi Face, gorgeous Jemima ♥ I love you ♥

Katie

WEDNESDAY 14th MARCH 2012

Jemima was declared dead, of an aneurism, at 4.28pm.

From Facebook:

Jemima, we have shared many memories these past 10 years, you were there for me when i couldn't confide in anyone else and it has meant so much to me; you are a kind, sensitive, clever and an amazing friend. You may be living with the angels but there will always be a place in my heart where I can remember those fun times we shared and the conversations we had; I will never forget you and you will be remembered as a truly amazing and lovable amigo, Freund, ami, amico, or rather, Friend. Farewell Jemima, after a long and faithful friendship I will never forget you; may your spirit linger on in all those who knew and loved you and may you rest in peace...

Treasured in my heart you'll stay, until we meet again someday,

Yours always,

Lauren

THURSDAY 15th MARCH 2012

How do I say goodbye without you?

How do I leave you?

When you've already gone.

How do I learn to fly without you?

When you were the one who urged me on.

How do I grab each day by the moment?

When you were the one who helped me grab on.

If you were the one who gave me my dreams,

How do I dream, when you are gone?

Lani

Oh Mima. I'm absolutely heartbroken. I loved you so, so much. You were like my sister. I'd known you for 13 whole years, and you were such a kind, bubbly, wacky, crazy, funny, silly, lovely girl to be around. Remember all those times we had. Dobby club, remember that? Oh Mima. I can't believe you're gone. How can I possibly look at a photo of you, all your wonderful letters you sent me without bleeding inside. It hurts so much that your life had to be robbed from you after just 13 years. You were so beautiful, I wish you could have known how special you were. You are in my thoughts always and I will NEVER EVER forget you. You were my bestest friend and even though you are gone I still feel you here with me now, and I know you can look down on me and see this message. I love you so much Mima. Goodbye. xxxxxxxxx ♥

Grace

SUNDAY 18th MARCH 2012

We were close friends

I believed you were sent from above

I knew I could count on you

For anything I needed

And when I needed you most

You were always there

I do miss our sleepovers

And the pranks you'd pull

And our long talks and

Our laughs we used to share

And how you made me feel better

Just by being there

I miss you my dearest loving friend

And I know you still care

We are friends forever and always

You and I
Friends till the end
Until the day I die
Wendy

Always and ever,
We will be,
Best of friends,
You and me.
I'm thinking of you every moment of every day. I've known you for as long as I can remember, and I'm simply too numbed to feel anything. I'm so shocked that the world could be so cruel as to take a beautiful angel like you.
But you live on through the happy memories we shared together. Remember the time I stayed at your house and Lauren told me there was an eagle looking through the window and I was so terrified your mum had to sit with me the whole night! That was just an example of the things we got up to. You were like a second sister to me and I cherished every moment with you, even if you did not think it. I hope you can look down from the safe place you are now in and acknowledge all I am saying. I hope you are at peace and my mum is looking after you. Xxxxxxx
Grace

Friends are forever, not just for lonely moments.
Friends have feelings, so treat them with respect.
Friends have days off, so try to understand them.
Be kind to everyone and accept it back.
Not everyone can be a friend but at least let them try.

Found this poem you wrote me. I'll never forget you ♥
Sophie

WEDNESDAY 21st MARCH 2012

Just can't come to terms with the fact that you are no longer with me, that I'll no longer see your beautiful face, stay up all night chatting when you have school the next day, and make fun of you when you write poems on the toilet! Oh Mima, you were so funny and I will have many fond memories of you that will stay with me 'til the day I die and beyond, I hope you are looking down on me now, and accept I am trying to get better as you would have wished. I love you xxxxxxxxxxxxxxxx ♥

Grace

EPILOGUE

We hope this diary helps you in several ways: firstly so that you can think for yourself whether organ donation is something you would like to do, secondly, so that you know you are not alone if you experience 'voices' in your head. It's important you talk to someone you trust about it and if you are worried visit your doctor. There is also a useful website: www.handsonscotland.co.uk

The voices, fainting and synaesthesia (mixed senses e.g. Hearing colours, seeing sounds) were not linked to her death at all. Fainting is something young teenage girls often experience, and many people are blessed with synaesthesia and enjoy the creative avenues it opens up.

A 5-year-old boy received Jemima's heart; a 14-year-old boy received her lungs. Her liver was split and shared between a 10-month-old baby boy and a 5-year-old boy. A 3 ½ year-old girl received a small bowel transplant and an adult female received her pancreas. A 24-year-old man and a 19-year-old man both received a kidney each. As well as her organs Jemima also donated her corneas, which in the future will give sight to two people, in addition to liver cells which were extracted for future use as an alternative to liver transplantation when patients are too sick to undergo a full transplant.

To register visit www.organdonation.nhs.uk
To find out more visit www.nhs.uk
Visit www.uksynaesthesia.com for more information.

APPENDIX

Report by Sophy Layzell to Mrs Bolland, housemistress, and Marie Andersen, counsellor, following events on Thursday 17th October 2011

What happened

1.	During Geography test 5th period Jemima wrote the following (see below) instead of answers to the last two questions.

2.	After a phone call from Sophy Layzell Jemima left Besley House and lay down in a circle of leaves behind the school buildings. Her friends and house mistress looked for her for an hour.

On finding her she wouldn't get up and said she wanted to stay, 'please I don't want to leave, I don't want the voices to come back,' the nurse helped her and carried her to the health centre where she rested, talked calmly, ate and then waited to be collected.

What J wrote

''I'm sorry I can't it hurts the voices too bad too much can't think can't hear they speak strange things always there talking why she left I don't know help me make the voices stop they scream they shout they don't make sense words thoughts faces everywhere the fire burns the clock ticks voices what's happening if he'd loved her would she still be here would she have jumped I'm sorry I can't concentrate too many voices please make them stop why do I see the faces why does no one else help me so confused I feel trapped inside someone else I don't expect anyone to understand how can they when even I don't understand oh no what have I done"

Both Harvey and I have had long talks with J since and want you to know the following.

What J says she feels

J has had experience of voices when she was little, but they stopped when she was about 7. Their return confused and panicked her.

(She has had 'blackouts' odd spells at the end of year 7 and we couldn't fully explain them but put them down to a combination of hormonal changes, heightened emotion, lack of food and dehydration.)

The voices are not threatening and in themselves are not frightening, but J is worried that hearing them is not normal and that people will think she's weird. The phone call from Sophy at 3.30pm made her worried that by talking or thinking about the voices they might come back. She describes it as 'if you ask someone to NOT think about penguins, then all they can think about Is . . . penguins!'

She left her house room to be on her own and find comfort. She has always loved trees and finds them peaceful. She had not realised how her actions would be interpreted. She did not mean to alarm and worry anyone. She does not have suicidal thoughts. She did not understand why she couldn't lie there.

We went through the written work line by line, trying to sift through it as there is no punctuation.

Talking about the writing we discovered...
1.   ''I'm sorry I can't it hurts the voices too bad too much can't think can't hear they speak strange things always there talking
This is in reaction to the voices that started at the end of the exam.
2.   why she left I don't know
This refers to Polly's suicide

3. help me make the voices stop they scream they shout they don't make sense words thoughts faces everywhere the fire burns the clock ticks voices what's happening

This is what the voices are saying. Mostly it's a blur of noise but some things are clear. Sometimes it's nonsense 'the apples are in the oven' for example.

4. if he'd loved her would she still be here would she have jumped

This refers to Polly's suicide

5. I'm sorry I can't concentrate too many voices please make them stop

She is aware she is in an exam and hasn't completed it.

6. why do I see the faces why does no one else help me so confused I feel trapped inside someone else

We explained that this is the section that we found most worrying.

She says she sees faces out of the corner of her eye, but that she can't see them if she looks directly at them. She finds the faces and voices confusing. She had a dream a few days ago, a life changing dream, which she doesn't want to tell us about, but now she feels different like 'someone else'

7. I don't expect anyone to understand how can they when even I don't understand

We have tried to reassure her that there may be a number of reasons why she experiences voices and that it's not unusual for children to hear them.

8. oh no what have I done

This is the realisation of what she has just written.

Our current position

We want J to feel confident in dealing with her voices and faces.

She realises that society will want her to have an acceptable reaction when they appear, so running off and not responding to adult help is not the way to deal with it.

If it happens again, she will ask her teachers if she can go to the medical centre, and tell Alice P who she would like to be her main confidante.

We have read that voices can occur:

1.   following trauma such as bereavement or abuse

2.   following problems with diet and hydration

We found www.handsonscotland.co.uk very useful

What we will do

We will ensure J has lots of slow and quick release energy snacks as she does have big energy crashes. She also cannot monitor how her body feels, and although hungry doesn't always recognise it, but she will make a big effort to keep her sugar levels up.

We are visiting her GP today 18.11.11. to have blood tests to check her sugar levels.

She is returning to school on Saturday and then having a night away with granny.

We will keep you both in the loop and value your support and opinion.

What we would like you to do

At school the medical centre has offered J refuge at any time should she need it. She needs to know she can arrive and ask to 'lie down because she's tired' and know that they will let her without questions.

If in class she needs to know that if she says 'I'm sorry but I feel ill please can I go to the medical centre' that she can without questions.

It would also be great if an older girl in Besley [30] could ensure J eats her snacks and that she doesn't feel obliged to share all of it!

---

[30] Jemima's school house.

Please read and use the above as reference for any further conversations. She doesn't wish to go through all her writing again, apparently that's like coming home and telling grandma all about her holiday and then having to repeat it all for granny!